HOW TO
DEFEND
THE FAITH

Without Raising Your Voice

CIVIL RESPONSES TO CATHOLIC HOT-BUTTON ISSUES

Austen Ivereigh
with John Norton

OUR SUNDAY VISITOR PUBLISHING DIVISION
OUR SUNDAY VISITOR, INC.
HUNTINGTON, INDIANA 46750

TABLE OF CONTENTS

INTRODUCTION

We know how it feels, finding yourself suddenly appointed the spokesman for the Catholic Church while you're standing at a photocopier, swigging a drink at the bar, or when a group of folks suddenly freezes, and all eyes fix on you.

"You're a Catholic, aren't you?" someone says.

"Um, yes," you confess, looking up nervously at what now seems to resemble a lynch mob.

The pope has been reported as saying something totally outrageous. Or the issue of AIDS and condoms has come up. Or the discussion has turned to gay marriage. And here you are, called on to defend the Catholic Church by virtue of your baptism, feeling as equipped for that task as Daniel in the den of lions.

"Go on," they seem to say, but don't actually put it that way. "Justify what the Church teaches!"

Scrabbling together a few thoughts, you put up a valiant defense, and people nod sympathetically. You contextualize, point out x and y, make a few observations they hadn't thought of, bring a little perspective into the question. The mob dissolves; people smile. They're not persuaded, but they don't want you to feel uncomfortable.

Or it didn't happen that way at all? Perhaps what happened was you got a little flustered and said a whole load of things which sounded pretty unpersuasive — even to you. You got irritated at the Church being constantly made to answer to a self-appointed inquisition of secular humanists and accused of bizarre conspiracies by people who had read too much Dan Brown. In fact, you became very flustered and flew off the handle; the feeling of persecution got to you. By the time you had spluttered out your angry defense, the gulf between you and everyone else had widened impossibly — and someone else had quickly, nervously, introduced a new topic.

Either way, here's what didn't happen. You didn't manage to "reframe" the issue. People still had the same view of the Church — dogmatic, authoritarian, anti-democratic, hypocritical, inhuman — as before you started speaking. You didn't turn the tables, recast the issue, open minds and hearts. You were stuck inside your opponent's frame.

As we were saying, we sympathize. It's not easy making the Church's case. The issues can be complex, and the headlines grotesquely simplistic. And it's hard to know, sometimes, what the Church's view actually is. Maybe you heard a bishop or theologian on the radio answering precisely that point. Maybe you've read up on it. But most likely, you just don't have the time to conduct major research on issues that keep coming up in conversations. You're bright and a committed Catholic. But you're also busy.

What you wish you had was an adviser, someone you could summon for a quick briefing, who could offer you (a) a bit of background, (b) a survey of the key issues, (c) some suggestions of how you might reframe the issue, and (d) some key points you could draw upon next time the question arises.

Well, here we are: not quite an adviser, but the next best thing — a book full of precisely such advice. Practical advice.

What you'll read in these pages is the result of a group of Catholics getting together to prepare themselves for precisely these high-pressure, get-to-the-heart-of-it-quick kind of contexts: not just around the water cooler, but in three-minute interviews on live television. Their experience, distilled here, will help you to "reframe" the hot-button issues which keep coming up in the news and provoke heated discussion.

We call these issues "neuralgic" because they touch on nerve endings, those places in the body which, when pressed, cause people to squeal. In our public conversation, they are the points which lie on the borders where mainstream social thinking inhabits (at least apparently) a different universe from that of Catholics. Touch on them, and people get very annoyed. "How on earth can you believe that?" they ask you.

Now, this book doesn't tell you what to say in answer to any given question. Every conversation is different. And it can't help you to know what's coming up in the news on a given day; not even the people who make the news can predict that. But chances are you'll be in a discussion sometime soon because of something involving the Church in the news, and most news stories involve one of those neuralgic issues. In fact, that's often what makes it a news story. Because of the perception in newsrooms that the Church's position on the question of condoms and AIDS is totally outrageous, when Pope Benedict XVI made a few off-the-cuff remarks about the issue in September 2009, it was a huge lead story across the globe. It wasn't the remarks so much as the neuralgic issue that made it news.

So while we can't predict the news story, we can be pretty sure about the neuralgic issues. This book will help you to think through ten of the most common (and the toughest) for yourself; to understand where the criticism is coming from; and to consider how to communicate the Church's position in ways that do not accept the presuppositions of the criticism. At the end of each of the nine briefing chapters, there are some "key messages" which summarize these positions — and will, we hope, help you next time you're challenged.

But there's a bit more to it than that. We'd better explain the method and approach used here, where it comes from, and what we're hoping to achieve.

This book is the fruit of a project called Catholic Voices, which was created for Pope Benedict XVI's visit to the United Kingdom in September 2010, and which has inspired similar groups in Spain, Ireland, Mexico, and other countries. A team of amateur speakers was formed, consisting of "ordinary" Catholics — in other words, Catholics who had jobs and children and mortgages — who were happy to put across Church positions and teaching on radio and television in the run-up to and during the papal visit. We are advertised to the media as "media-friendly, studio-ready and ego-free," by which we meant: happy to be questioned, and sympathetic to the media's objectives and reason for existing; familiar with the demands of three-minute live interviews, and the constraints and possibilities of radio and TV; and uncomplaining if the news has moved on and you no longer need us. We were described as "authoritative but not official": we set out to be well briefed and articulate, knowledgeable, and able to communicate the settled teachings of the Church. But while we had the blessing of the bishops, we did not speak for them. If you wanted to know how the bishops responded to such and such a story in today's news, you would need to call their spokespeople. But if you wanted to know what the Church believed and taught, you could call us.

The project was a success. The individuals of Catholic Voices were in dozens of debates and news programs on radio and TV, appearing on all the major British channels, and winning the praise of bishops and broadcasters alike.

Perhaps the most important fruit of the Catholic Voices experience was the "method" we developed in the many intensive briefings we held in the months before the pope arrived, one that we think works for anyone who needs to make the Church's case — not just in a three-minute live TV interview, but also in a three-minute live bar conversation, or a half-hour lunch-break discussion provoked by an item on the news. After all, the two situations are not so different. If you can't say it quickly, compellingly, and sound like a human being, then you've lost people's interest and sympathy. That may not be a disaster, but it's certainly a missed opportunity.

What we learned was a particular mind-set, one that helped us to avoid being defensive or aggressive, which was vital to enable us to "reframe" the criticism. We've summed up that approach in a series of principles which may be a means of reviving the art of apologetics for our age — an era of 24-hour news. Those principles are listed in the last chapter so you can look at them anytime you're about to enter an environment in which you'll be challenged.

At the heart of this approach is what we call "positive intention." Behind every criticism of the Church, however apparently hostile or prejudiced, is an ethical value. The critic is consciously or unconsciously appealing to that value. Issues become neuralgic, in fact, precisely because of the feeling that those core values are threatened. Surprisingly, perhaps, the value behind the criticism is one you might recognize as being valid — Christian, even — or at least derived from a Christian value.

That's not so astonishing, given that we live in Christian — or some might say "post-Christian" — cultures. What secularization means is that people abandon the Church yet continue, unconsciously, to adhere to its values — and often appeal (again unconsciously) to those values when they criticize the Church. It is much easier to persuade the critic if you can appeal to that same value, or show that you agree with it. At the same time, you will be less defensive. Empathy is the beginning of dialogue. Dialogue does not mean abandoning or adjusting your values, but building relationships of trust between people of differing convictions. This book teaches the art of that dialogue: not how to defend positions, but to explain them and to enable others to understand them.

By looking at the positive intention behind the criticism we were able to get out of the mind-set of, "How can I justify this?" and instead ask, "What is the real source of the disagreement here?" For example: The desire for an assisted-suicide law is based on the positive intention that people should be spared unnecessary suffering. Now we, as Catholics, agree that while suffering is inevitable in aging and dying, no one should experience unbearable pain and loneliness, which is why many of the hospices specializing in palliative care have been founded and are run by Catholics. So now that we can agree on that, we can then look at where we disagree — the meaning of death, the question of autonomy, etc. — and then look at the practical issue of what an assisted-suicide law would mean for health care, for the view of the elderly, and so on. The discussion can become more rational and constructive because we are not arguing with people from another planet but those who are part of our same culture of values.

That is why early in each of the chapters you'll find a small section featuring the positive intention behind the criticism. It will help put you in the mind-set of the critic — and realize that we have a job of explaining to do. You can move away from being threatened by him or her and instead think, "How do we get this across?"

At the beginning of each chapter, you'll also see a list of "challenging questions." As we said, no one can predict exactly what questions will be asked about a particular neuralgic issue. News stories vary. Yet because the neuralgic issues remain constant, the questions are reasonably predictable. The individuals of Catholic Voices were amazed to find that the questions they faced in studios were almost always variations of the ones we had considered in the briefings. That's because the positive intention behind the criticism generates a series of natural questions. But don't think our challenging questions are in any way exhaustive. You'll easily add some of your own.

Now that we've explained something of our approach, we'd like a word about scandal — and to issue an invitation from Pope Benedict XVI.

The Catholic faith "scandalizes." It causes people to react strongly and ask hard questions. Thank God for that. It's what the Gospel does. "Blessed is he that shall not be scandalized in me," says Jesus, referring to those who do not turn away in disgust or miscomprehension (Mt 11:6, Douay-Rheims). But it's Jesus, of course, who lays down the stumbling blocks — the *skandala*, as they're called in Greek. A *skandalon* is an obstacle in the path. It causes people to stop and think; their existing frame is threatened. And this can be the start of another path, one that leads, potentially, to a new way of looking at something. Or it can lead to the "turning away" of which Jesus warns.

That turning away — that furious rejection — is the enemy of true communication. Yet just before that point, when people are scandalized and ask questions — even if the questions are in the form of angry accusations — they have not yet turned away; they are open to hearing another view. That is why every tough question in a radio and TV interview, every animated discussion over a beer, every awkward dinner-party moment, is an opportunity. Is this evangelization? We see it more as "clearing the obstacles to evangelization." It's clarifying misunderstanding, shedding light where there is myth and confusion. It can cause people to reconsider their objections to what the Church says. Whatever we want to call it — "apologetics," "communication" — it's a witness, and a vital one.

In media news terms, it's getting in at the beginning, to reframe the story as it's breaking. Some call this "spin-doctoring," a term dating to the 1980s that is discredited because it suggests the dark arts of media manipulation. That's why we prefer the term "reframing." Reframing tells a different story from what's out there. It's not a disreputable or manipulative thing to do if what you are doing is telling the truth: indeed, reframing works only if what you're saying is true. "False ideas may be refuted indeed by argument," said Blessed Cardinal John Henry Newman, our lodestar in this enterprise, "but by true ideas alone are they expelled."

This is a witness. It's also a vocation. And here's the invitation. We're hoping that this book helps "ordinary" Catholics — that's probably you we're talking about here — to see themselves as communicators. Some people (again this may be you) have a natural gift for this. They are the kind of people who love to gnaw on an issue, or the kind of person who loves to clarify and build bridges. There are many kinds of Catholic communicators: some delight in concepts, others speak out of experience; some are impassioned orators; others are gentle, thoughtful types. But they are all motivated by a desire to put across their faith in human, compelling ways; and a bit impatient to get out there and correct some of the frustrating misapprehensions they hear every day about the Church they love.

No one is excluded from this calling, but it is pre-eminently a mission for laypeople, as Pope Benedict said in his homily in Glasgow after arriving in Scotland:

> I appeal in particular to you, the lay faithful, in accordance with your baptismal calling and mission, not only to be examples of faith in public, but also to put the case for the promotion of faith's wisdom and vision in the public forum.

In a January 2012 address to the U.S. bishops, Pope Benedict repeated that call. Warning of the pressure from a new radical secularism and the threats to freedom of religion, he asked for Catholics to step up to meet those challenges:

> Here once more we see the need for an engaged, articulate, and well-formed Catholic laity endowed with a strong critical sense vis-à-vis the dominant culture and with the courage to counter a reductive secularism which would delegitimize the Church's participation in public debate about the issues which are determining the future of American society. The preparation of committed lay leaders and the presentation of a convincing articulation of the Christian vision of man and society remain a primary task of the Church in your country.

This is a task bigger than "defending the Church." In his response to the pope's address, Archbishop José Gomez of Los Angeles said:

> Now is a time for Catholic action and for Catholic voices. We need lay leaders to step up to their responsibilities for the Church's mission, not only to defend our faith and our rights as Catholics, but to be leaders for moral and civic renewal — leaders in helping to shape the values and moral foundations of America's future.

It's about learning to articulate what is a treasure for the whole of society — the value of religious freedom, from which all other freedoms flow; an authentic pluralism which allows for a vigorous civil society based on strong families and committed marriages; and the building blocks of "an authentically just, humane and prosperous society," in Pope Benedict's words. It means, as he also said, "proposing rational arguments in the public square"; applying the insights of the great social encyclicals; highlighting the needs of the poor and the disadvantaged; calling for virtue in public life and the building of institutions; and helping to define a better relationship between state, market, and civil society. It's about advancing a vision of society that defends life — however feeble or invisible — and the dignity of every human being. It's about helping to build a civilization of love.

Hence the need for Catholics who — to use Blessed Cardinal Newman's phrase — "know their creed so well that they can give an account of it." The public square is, to a very large extent, defined by the media. That's where the chatter of the marketplace is to be found; and it's where Catholics need to learn to be at home, speaking succinctly and compellingly of their Church's vision. But the public square is also where *you* are, where you meet and interact with others in the many crossroads of contemporary society.

Actors and writers often talk about finding their voice — that moment when the character they've been working hard at creating comes alive and hits the right notes. That's something the Church always needs to do, in each generation: to find its voice in society. And it's something every Catholic is called to do — in the media, yes, but also in the workplace, among friends, and at those dinner parties which suddenly fall awkwardly silent.

We hope this book will help you find that voice.

Chapter 1

THE CHURCH AND POLITICAL LIFE

— Challenging Questions —

- *Why does the Church interfere in politics? Shouldn't it just keep to religion?*
- *Why does it try to control Catholics in the way that they vote — and to pressure Catholic politicians on questions such as abortion?*
- *What right does the Church have to interfere in the laws of secular states?*
- *Is it a Church or a state? Why does it act like a state?*

The Catholic Church has often been accused of "meddling" in politics. Rulers (and sometimes voters) resent being held to account by a higher law. In the age of democracy, the accusation is sometimes levied against the Church that it acts as a kind of lobby, using its spiritual influence to engineer certain political outcomes — acting, in other words, out of corporate self-interest. Critics accuse the Church of "imposing its view" on the rest of society in an attempt to thwart human rights — usually understood narrowly and one-sidedly as those of a woman to seek an abortion or a gay couple to adopt a child.

A specific neuralgic issue is the Vatican's status as a state, or rather, the international influence of the Holy See, the seat of governance of the Church worldwide. In the weeks before Pope Benedict XVI's visit to the United Kingdom in September 2010, the "Protest the Pope" coalition objected that, if the pope was a faith leader, why was he being received as a state visitor? Surely, the protesters argued, the state of which he is head (Vatican City) is a tiny and insignificant territory — the result of a sordid pact with the fascist dictator Benito Mussolini in 1929.

At the same time as critics sought to downplay the Vatican's status as a state, they also exaggerated it, accusing the Vatican of throwing its diplomatic weight around internationally, lobbying at the United Nations, and frustrating "progressive" policies around the world by teaming up with Muslims, for example, against "women's rights."

Domestically, the Church is accused of interfering in the democratic process in a number of ways: by "telling Catholics how to vote" at elections; by lobbying governments, bringing to bear its corporate influence on Congress; and by coercing Catholic politicians into voting according to the Church's dictates under threat of denying them Communion.

☙

POSITIVE INTENTION

The positive value behind criticism of the Church as a "self-interested" lobby is that it should be promoting and be driven by the common good, rather than narrow self-interest. The criticism correctly assumes that the Church is founded on another kind of power — covenant relationships, the fruit of communion — and that those who proclaim God should not need to make use of "the means of this world" to promote God, because Truth persuades on its own merits. Behind the criticism, therefore, is an implicitly Christian view of the Church itself — even if it is a little unreal. True, the Church is not like a corporation. But nor is it disembodied, floating above the world; it is an institution thoroughly in the world, seeking to shape it while looking to a transcendent horizon. Another positive value in the criticism is that the Church should stand for progress in human history, not seek to block it.

☙

Temporal vs. Spiritual

The attempt to drive religion out of politics does not have a happy history. The greatest horrors of the twentieth century were inflicted by totalitarian states among whose first moves was the abolition of faith from the public sphere and the subordination of religion to the state. Conversely, some of the proudest moments of Western political history — the abolition of the slave trade, or the civil-rights movement of the 1950s and 1960s — are uplifting examples of what happens when religion enters politics. The greatest achievements in Western history are products of a civilization in which Church and state cooperate, and reason and faith are in dialogue. The greatest disasters have arisen from efforts by the state to eradicate the Church, often justified by an ideology which interprets the "will of the people" as a license for unchecked, unlimited power.

The Second Vatican Council renounced the idea of the Church seeking special privileges from the state. Its *Dignitatis Humanae* (Declaration on Religious Freedom) was a bitter pill for some in countries where the Church had long confused "Catholic society" with "Catholic state." But these were atypical; Christianity is essentially anti-theocratic. The examples of the Church being too close to the state, when faith has been subordinated to party politics, when witness has been diminished and corrupted, are lessons from which the modern Church has learned.

Christianity believes in keeping the two spheres of faith and politics apart, yet interconnected. Unlike secularism, which proclaims the moral autonomy of the state, a healthy or positive secularity advocates a distinction between faith and politics (but not their divorce). The precise relationship of faith and politics, spiritual and temporal, is a complex one, and there are many different models: the French, the Americans, the British, and the Italians, for example, all have contrasting ways of keeping Church and state both distinct and in relationship. But the underlying principle should be clear. On the one hand, reason and religion need each other; they are inextricably bound together. On the other, they are distinct realms and should not be confused, for the sake of both the Church and the state. Put simply, not every sin should be a crime, and not every crime a sin.

Those who resent the Church "interfering" in politics often object to the perceived politics behind the "interference," rather than the interference itself. Thus the Church is criticized as reactionary or right wing for opposing "women's rights" (in arguing against liberal abortion laws) or for being against "gay rights" (when it opposes, say, same-sex adoption). But the Church is also regularly criticized for being left wing in economic and social matters — as when it advocates a pathway to citizenship for long-term migrants or when it opposes the death penalty. So really the accusation against the Church for being either right or left wing tells you more about contemporary political assumptions than about the political inclination of Catholicism. The Church will seem both "right wing" (in promoting the traditional family, opposing abortion, euthanasia, embryonic research, etc.) *and* "left wing" (in advocating the rights of minorities, social justice, active state support for the poorest, etc.), depending on the political bias of the one accusing. The same bias afflicts Catholics. There are pro-life Catholics who think Catholic social teaching is "socialist," and pro-social-justice Catholics who think pro-life causes are right wing.

The Church will always be accused of "interfering" or trying to "impose" its view when the critic disagrees with its stance; but the same critic will say nothing when the Church has intervened politically on a matter with which he or she agrees. And if the Church has stayed silent, the critic will accuse it of "failing to speak out." Put another way, people are against the Church "interfering" in what they would much rather have left alone; and in favor of "interfering" in what they believe should be changed.

The Church's Right to Speak Out

Why and when does the Church speak out on political questions? The answer is rarely and cautiously, and almost always because it is a matter which touches on the Gospel, on core freedoms and rights (such as the right to life, or to religious freedom), or on core principles of Catholic social teaching. In these cases, the Church not only needs to speak out; it has a *duty* to do so.

The Church promotes active citizenship and political engagement. Christians have always understood themselves to be dual citizens — simultaneously members of the Church and of political society — who must obey the law and work for the good of the Kingdom wherever they are, whatever regime they are under. This "dual citizenship" is not a divided loyalty — Catholics are both loyal citizens of their countries *and* loyal to Rome — but it does produce a healthful tension. Living in the world while looking to a transcendent horizon produces a tension which is extremely healthy for a democracy, and is one reason Catholics are unusually active in politics.

Within certain limits (racist parties, for example, are off limits) Catholics are free to vote for whomever they wish; as a body, the Church avoids partisanship — favoring one political party over another — while reserving the right to speak out when a core value is at stake, and encouraging Catholics to enter the political process, to help make society a better place.

In a modern democracy the Church claims its right to speak out for the same reason that any other civil-society association or organization does — a natural right to proclaim and promote its values, and to persuade others of these; to get a debate going about the health of society and its priorities, applying the wisdom and insights of the Christian tradition to the great questions besetting contemporary society. The Church does this because it cares, above all, for the "common good," described by the *Catechism of the Catholic Church* as "the sum total of social conditions which allow people, either as groups or as individuals, to reach their fulfilment more fully and more easily" (no. 1906). The common good is a key tenet of the Church's vision for society and the principles which it believes lie behind its healthy functioning.

The argument that the Church doesn't speak for the majority is true as far as it goes (which is not very far: nearly 80 percent of Americans self-identify as Christian, and 25 percent as Catholics). But the Church's right to speak out has never been dependent on the numbers of its followers. Nor when it advocates or criticizes is the Church trying to "impose" its view — although, like others with strong views in a democratic society, it seeks to persuade others. On the other hand, the Church can claim to represent substantial numbers of American citizens, as well as being the world's, and the United States', largest practicing Christian body, and the most significant civil-society actor on the world stage. It speaks out of a tradition which shaped the moral and cultural values of the Western world. And because it is politically and nationally independent, it can ask questions of society that others are not prepared to ask, and speak for those deprived of a voice.

A Global Actor

With nearly 1.2 billion adherents — about one-fifth of the world's population — the Church is the world's oldest and largest organization, present through more than 400,000 priests, 800,000 religious sisters, and 219,655 parishes. It is the world's second largest international development body (after the United Nations), and the second largest humanitarian agency (after the Red Cross). Caritas Internationalis, the sixty-year-old Rome-based confederation of 165 national bodies of Catholic charities in more than 200 countries, estimates their combined annual budget at over $5 billion. In Africa the Church runs a quarter of all the hospitals, and its schools educate around 12 million children each year. Globally, it runs more than 5,000 hospitals, 17,500 dispensaries, and 15,000 homes for the elderly, along with tens of thousands of schools. As well as laying claim to being the world's leading moral teacher and guide — an "expert in humanity," as the Vatican's Pontifical Council for Justice and Peace puts it — the Catholic Church is the largest and most influential actor in global civil society.

Like other global players, it has "international policy objectives." The Catholic Church is the only religious body to have an official presence — that of Observer Status — at the United Nations. It is the only religion with a diplomatic corps (the oldest still in existence). But then, the Church is a uniquely significant institution.

Worldwide, the Church is a crucial backer of the Millennium Development Goals (MDGs), the United Nation's global action plan, and a tireless promoter of debt cancellation and other forms of financial aid to the developing world. The Vatican is the world's first carbon-neutral state. The Holy See plays a crucial role in disarmament negotiations and arms-trade treaties, in campaigning against the death penalty worldwide, in negotiating the release of hostages, and in conflict resolution. And it advocates reforms designed to place the economy more at the service of humanity. In 2011, for example, the Pontifical Council for Justice and Peace called for new global structures capable of restraining and regulating the international financial markets for the sake of the common good, backing in particular the idea of a tax on financial transactions.

These might all be considered "progressive" initiatives, but the Church would also regard as progressive its opposition to embryonic stem-cell research, abortion laws, and gay marriage. It would see as progressive its opposition to euthanasia and assisted suicide, as well as its opposition to the death penalty and its advocacy — around the world, including in the United States — of a pathway to citizenship for "illegal" immigrants who have put down roots in another country. What all these issues have in common is the defense of the dignity of the human person, even if that dignity is not recognized by wider society, because the persons concerned (the unborn, children, the elderly, prisoners, foreign-born) are not seen as "human beings like us"; or when the rights of particular groups (victims of crime, pregnant women, same-sex couples) are seen as in some way absolute or nullifying the rights of others.

Vatican or Holy See?

Vatican City is a magnificent (if small) area in Rome recognized as a state as a result of the 1929 Lateran Pacts. The agreement signed with the Italian dictator Benito Mussolini brought to an end a long-running question over the Vatican's territorial sovereignty following the loss of the Papal States and Italy's birth as a nation-state. It is sometimes claimed that the Vatican is recognized internationally as a state only because of that "sordid pact with a dictator." But this is to confuse two different things: the Vatican's status as a state, and the international sovereign jurisdiction of the Holy See, which has been recognized for centuries, long before the creation of the Vatican City State.

The diplomatic ties which the United States and other states maintain with the Catholic Church worldwide were not and are not contingent in any way upon the Lateran Pact. Britain's oldest diplomatic relationship, for example, is with the Holy See — first established formally in 1479, and re-established in 1914, many years before the Pact. The United States had consular relations with the Papal States from 1797 under President George Washington, but ties were interrupted in 1870 in large part because of national anti-Catholic sentiment. In 1984, President Ronald Reagan established diplomatic relations and named the first U.S. ambassador to the Holy See.

The Holy See is the seat of governance of the worldwide Catholic Church. It has international sovereign jurisdiction, meaning that it is recognized as a legal entity, with which governments have relations. This sovereignty is what enables, for example, the bishop of a local diocese to be appointed by the Vatican, rather than by the local government. This gives the Church an important degree of independence from political power. Autocratic governments such as China's refuse to accept Rome's right to appoint bishops, regarding it as interference in its sovereign affairs. Religious freedom — the freedom to worship, manifest one's belief, and so on — is safeguarded by the Catholic Church's independence, manifest in its international sovereignty.

Much of what the Holy See achieves worldwide — the result of bringing its moral authority and global presence to bear on countries to help effect change — is possible because of this sovereign international jurisdiction. It means that countries can have formal diplomatic ties with it — just under 200 states do — which in turn means that the

Catholic Church can exert its moral influence to make the world a better place. The Holy See has had a continuous history as an organization since the fourth century, which makes it older than most nation-states. Nor is that relationship one restricted to Catholic countries. Among the many things Western diplomats find useful about their links to the Vatican are the Holy See's relationships of trust with nations (Iran, for example) with which the United States has broken political ties. The Vatican's international diplomatic network — the fruit of patient, behind-the-scenes trust-building across the globe — is a vital resource for world peace and cooperation.

The Church's Presence in the United States

When the Church raises its voice in U.S. domestic affairs, it does so by virtue of its moral authority, its independent sovereign jurisdiction, and its strong presence in American civil society. The 78 million Catholics in the United States represent 25 percent of the population. Nor is this affiliation nominal or passive; the Center for Applied Research in the Apostolate at Georgetown University reports that 44 percent of the Catholic population — 34.3 million — goes to Mass at least once a month, demonstrating, by the standards of contemporary society, a highly unusual level of engagement and commitment.

They show that commitment in countless other ways. Practicing Catholics play a disproportionately large role in voluntary organizations, welfare agencies, and education, and are more likely than the general population to volunteer in every age group. The Church runs 7,000 schools and 18,000 parishes; there are 44,000 priests and 56,000 female religious; but the "Church" is also those hundreds of thousands of Catholics who give their time, talents, and money to a huge number of associations of every kind working for the common good.

The Catholic charitable sector in the United States is a massive contributor to the common good of the nation, conspicuous at the fringes of society, caring for those whom society has either left behind or scorns: the elderly, the disabled, children, young offenders, the homeless, migrants without papers, seafarers, persons with AIDS, prisoners, alcoholics, drug addicts, prostitutes… The list is almost endless.

Catholics reach out to the poorest and most vulnerable irrespective of their beliefs. As many Catholics say, "We care for the poor not because they are Catholics, but because we are." Catholic charitable action is strictly not proselytizing: as Pope Benedict XVI says in *Deus Caritas Est* ("God Is Love"), "Those who practice charity in the Church's name will never seek to impose the Church's faith upon others." At the same time, there is no greater witness to Christ's love than to serve the poor both through practical, direct assistance and through advocacy on their behalf, often at the cost of upsetting and challenging existing assumptions and values.

A recent annual report of Catholic Charities USA, the umbrella of Catholic charities in dioceses across the United States, shows that some 337,000 employees and volunteers serve more than 9 million people, spending some $4 billion every year. But it's not just the scale of the Catholic charitable contribution that matters, but the unique way it serves the common good of society.

Catholic charities often do what no one else does, blazing a trail where others later follow. There are countless examples of charitable outreach pioneered by Catholics which over time become "mainstream" charitable activities; hospices caring for the terminally ill are a prime example. Others remain preserves of the Church. No organization compares with the Apostleship of the Sea, which provides support and assistance to hundreds of thousands of seafarers visiting U.S. ports each year.

Although ultimately inspired by the Gospel — not least the parable of the Good Samaritan and Jesus' words in Matthew 25 — most of these charities are directly motivated by the example of a charismatic founder, often a saint. They grow directly out of civil society (rather than as a creation of the state), and frequently depend on and work through parishes and schools, galvanizing the energies and passions of networks of volunteers. (Members of the St. Vincent de Paul Society USA, for example, spend 7 million hours each year attending to the socially excluded. The Knights of Columbus volunteer more than 70 million hours annually in charitable causes.).

Finally, Catholics are guided by a coherent set of principles, embodied in Catholic social teaching, which in turn enrich American social and political thinking and strengthen civil society. Through nationwide organizations, Catholic charities advocate on behalf of those they serve, influencing policy decisions and helping to shape laws which serve the interests of the poor.

American Catholics also make a massive contribution to overseas development and humanitarian relief through the bishops' agency Catholic Relief Services. Founded in 1943 to help resettle war refugees in Europe after World War II, CRS now spends more than $800 million annually, working with hundreds of active partners worldwide — usually the local Church — to tackle international poverty, and influencing global decisions through its membership in the Vatican-based Caritas Internationalis. CRS is consistently a top-ranked charity, with an A+ rating from the American Institute of Philanthropy.

The United States Conference of Catholic Bishops in Washington, D.C., with an annual budget of more than $215 million, employs a number of full-time public-policy officers to develop links between the Church and federal lawmakers and officials. The bishops conference president is regularly invited to the Oval Office for a meeting with the president of the United States. There is nothing unusual or sinister about this. Many large organizations which lay claim to a significant influence over sectors of public opinion — trade unions, faiths, newspapers, business associations, and so on — are regularly consulted by government, and can expect to be listened to when laws are being formulated that could affect the lives of those these organizations represent. It would be a very poor and authoritarian government which regarded its electoral majority as a mandate to govern without consultation.

Meanwhile, there are about 150 Catholic members of Congress, representing nearly 30 percent of the total. The number of Catholic Republicans nearly equals the number of Catholic Democrats.

Bishops and Elections

Every so often, generally well in advance of a general election, the U.S. Catholic bishops issue a document setting out some of the considerations they believe voters should keep in mind when they cast their ballot. They are *not* advocating one particular party or another; their aim is instead to influence all parties and their platforms — and to mobilize the electorate to take a clear interest in their local candidates. (As it happens, the Catholic vote swings between the two major parties). In politics, it is normal to seek to persuade others of your vision; everyone in politics is, in that sense, trying to "impose" his or her values by the force of persuasion.

In 2011, the bishops decided to re-release their 2007 document "Forming Consciences for Faithful Citizenship" with a fresh introductory note. While the note doesn't modify the document itself, it raises six "current and fundamental problems, some involving opposition to intrinsic evils and others raising serious moral questions."

They are: abortion and threats to the lives and dignity of the vulnerable, sick, or unwanted; threats to Catholic ministries, including health care, education, and social services, to violate their consciences or stop serving those in need; intensifying efforts to redefine marriage; unemployment, poverty, and debt; immigration; and wars, terror, and violence, particularly in the Middle East.

In "Faithful Citizenship," the bishops identify seven key themes of Catholic social teaching:

1. "The dignity of the human person is the foundation of a moral vision for society." Thus the Church's stance on abortion, euthanasia, human cloning, destructive embryonic research, torture, unjust war, the death penalty, genocide and racism.
2. "The family — based on marriage between a man and a woman — is the first and fundamental unit of society and is a sanctuary for the creation and nurturing of children."
3. "Human dignity is respected and the common good is fostered only if human rights are protected and basic responsibilities are met."
4. "While the common good embraces all, those who are weak, vulnerable, and most in need deserve preferential concern. A basic moral test for our society is how we treat the most vulnerable in our midst."
5. "The economy must serve people, not the other way around."
6. "We are one human family, whatever our national, racial, ethnic, economic, and ideological differences. We are our brothers' and sisters' keepers, wherever they may be."
7. "Care for the earth is a duty of our faith and a sign of our concern for all people."

Church, Conscience, and Politicians

Another objection to the Church's involvement in the political sphere is that it threatens Catholic politicians with excommunication if they fail to "toe the line" on questions such as abortion. In this way, say critics, the Church interferes in the democratic process, seeking to "impose its view" through the use of a kind of moral coercion. But this is to look at it the wrong way. The Church has to maintain its internal good order, and one of the obligations of bishops is to act to make clear when Church teaching on vital questions is being misrepresented by people in public positions in such a way as risks misleading the faithful.

The issue has arisen specifically in the case of abortion and euthanasia because these are concerned with the sanctity of life, which the Church believes should be reflected in society's rule of law, defending "the basic right to life from conception to natural death." This right holds a "unique place" in Catholic social teaching, notes the prefect of the Congregation for the Doctrine of the Faith, U.S. Cardinal William J. Levada, so that "there may be legitimate diversity of opinion even among Catholics about waging war and applying the death penalty, but not with regard to abortion and euthanasia." In order for a Catholic to be in full communion with the faith of the Church, therefore, he or she must accept this teaching; referring to laws which promote or authorize abortion and euthanasia, Pope John Paul II's encyclical letter *Evangelium Vitae* ("The Gospel of Life") says there is "a grave and clear obligation to oppose them by conscientious objection" (no. 73).

What should the Church do about politicians who advertise themselves as Catholics but who vote time and again to liberalize abortion laws, or to undermine attempts at restricting those laws? In January 2004, when the Democrat presidential candidate John Kerry was campaigning in his diocese, the then-archbishop of St. Louis, Mo., now Cardinal Raymond Burke, announced he would refuse the candidate Communion. Kerry was a Massgoer, but he also had a notoriously pro-abortion voting record, and Archbishop Burke wanted to make clear that these two things were incompatible. Archbishop Burke's stance was supported by some U.S. bishops, but it was resisted by others, including Kerry's own bishop, Cardinal Seán O'Malley of Boston, who were anxious not to politicize the Eucharist.

In the end the bishops met in June 2004 and agreed to disagree. "Given the wide range of circumstances involved in arriving at a prudential judgment" on the question, their statement read, "bishops can legitimately make different judgments on the most prudent course of pastoral action. Such decisions," the statement concluded, "rest with the individual bishop in accord with established canonical and pastoral principles."

Their statement, "Catholics in Political Life," was issued after the reading of a memorandum by the prefect of the Congregation for the Doctrine of the Faith, then-Cardinal Joseph Ratzinger (who later became Pope Benedict XVI). In it he advised U.S. bishops to speak *privately* with prominent Catholics who defy Church teachings on key issues involving the sanctity of life, alert them to the gravity of their offenses, and warn them that they will be refused Communion if they do not change their ways. Only if these warnings are not heeded, Cardinal Ratzinger added, "and the person in question, with obstinate persistence, still presents himself to receive the holy Eucharist, the minister of holy Communion must refuse to distribute it."

The issue for the bishops, in other words, was not how to influence the outcome of an election or a politician's voting record, but how to deal with a particular scandal arising from a public Catholic who was publicly violating Church teaching in an essential matter of ethics. It was precisely because Archbishop Burke's stance risked influencing how Catholics might vote that some other bishops were reluctant to follow his example. Cardinal Ratzinger's solution reflected this concern; he advocated the public disbarring from Communion only as a matter of last resort. The Church upholds as an important first principle that political battles should be fought, in the words of the archbishop of Washington at the time, Cardinal Theodore McCarrick, "not at the Communion rail but in the public square, in hearts and minds, in our pulpits and public advocacy, in our consciences and communities."

What the Church Stands For

It is up to Catholics involved in politics to make up their own minds about which parties to support, and why. Their priorities and concerns will differ; so will their loyalties and their affiliations. But there are key principles on which all Catholics should agree because they have been consistently taught by the Church since 1891 when Pope Leo XIII issued the first "social encyclical" of modern times: *Rerum Novarum* (on capital and labor). Since then, there have been many more encyclicals — the latest is Pope Benedict XVI's *Caritas in Veritate* ("Charity in Truth") — and many other Church documents expanding on and applying these principles to contemporary challenges. Catholic social teaching (CST) offers a set of principles for reflection, criteria for judgment, and directives for action. Its purpose is to contribute to the formation of conscience as a basis for specific action. It amounts, in effect, to a Catholic vision of politics, society, and the economy.

CST, which came into being in response to the development of modern Western capitalism, has two major concerns. The first is the alienation between capital and labor — the division of society into those who control wealth and property, and the majority who have to sell their labor. (It was the growth of the poverty-stricken masses in the cities of Europe which sparked Pope Leo's encyclical). The second is the growth in the power of the market and the state, and the reduction in the size and the strength of civil society. Put positively, the popes in seventeen key social encyclicals since 1891 have urged two essential reforms to the modern liberal market polity and economy. The first is the "humanization" of the market, putting people before profits, and remembering the human purpose of the economy. The second is a call for a strengthened civil society made up of vigorous "intermediate associations," as opposed to a society seen as made up only of the state, capital, and isolated individuals.

CST has a number of key principles set out in a series of papal encyclicals and other Church documents over time: the dignity of the human person, the common good, a just wage, the universal destination of goods, solidarity, subsidiarity, participation, option for the poor, peace and disarmament, the preservation of life and creation, and the call to action. Each of these themes is a rich mine of insight and wisdom into the right ordering of a modern, democratic, pluralist society.

The Catholic political agenda is also marked by its strong advocacy of religious freedom, considered by the Church to be the first and most fundamental of all basic rights, from which all others flow. The enemies of religious freedom are both fundamentalism and secularism. "The same determination that condemns every form of fanaticism and religious fundamentalism must also oppose every form of hostility to religion that would restrict the public role of believers in civil and political life," said Pope Benedict in his January 1, 2011, Peace Day message. "Religious fundamentalism and secularism are alike in that both represent extreme forms of a rejection of legitimate pluralism and the principle of secularity."

Religious freedom is not just immunity from coercion in matters of conscience — the freedom to reject faith and God, or to convert from one faith to another. It is also, says Pope Benedict, "the ability to order one's own choices in accordance with truth." The recognition of this freedom is the bedrock of pluralism and democracy because it implies that God and conscience precede the state. The state, with its coercive power, is not the arbiter of consciences, conceding rights, but at the service of a society made up of many different ideas about truth. What undermines religious freedom, therefore, is what distorts the delicate balance between temporal and spiritual, leading to the eclipse of one by the other, which in turn produces (eventually) fundamentalism enthroned in theocracy, or relativism enthroned in totalitarianism. As Pope Benedict said in his address to United Kingdom lawmakers in September 2010: "The world of reason and the world of faith — the world of secular rationality and the world of religious belief — need one another and should not be afraid to enter into profound and ongoing dialogue, for the good of our civilization."

ʘ

EXISTING FRAME

"The Catholic Church uses its power and influence to advance a reactionary agenda designed to frustrate progress in human rights and liberties. Bishops tell people how to vote and threaten politicians with excommunication when they don't do the pope's bidding. The Church is essentially right wing, seeking to impose outdated views on a secular state and on people who have no Christian allegiance."

REFRAME

The Church raises its voice in the public sphere whenever an issue touches on the common good, often on questions of basic freedoms and rights, and especially when it can be a voice for the voiceless. Its authority to speak out derives from its moral authority and independence as one of the world's leading and oldest civil-society organizations. It is neither right nor left wing and has no allegiance to particular political parties, but exists to defend the common good and the Gospel in its integrity. It defends, and speaks up for, a distinction between the political and the religious; it upholds what it calls a "positive secularity" and deplores both religious fundamentalism and an aggressive kind of secularism which seeks to banish faith from the public square. When it deplores politicians who claim to be Catholic while advocating, for example, abortion and euthanasia, it is not trying to coerce politicians but to prevent scandal. The Catholic Church's political agenda can be summed up as Catholic social teaching plus religious freedom, the freedom which underlies all other rights and freedoms.

Key Messages

- The Church has a natural right to speak out derived from its moral authority and its presence in society.
- The Church advocates religious freedom and the proper distinction between faith and politics. At the same time it calls for the political and the religious to be in dialogue, not separated.
- Bishops do not speak out before elections to persuade Catholics to vote one way or another; they identify the issues they think Catholics should be concerned about, and which voters should be asking the candidates to address.
- The Catholic Church's political agenda can be summed up in Catholic social teaching and religious freedom. It is an agenda which is the bedrock of freedom and civilization.

Chapter 2

HOMOSEXUALITY AND CONTRACEPTION

— Challenging Questions —

- *Why is the Church in favor of family planning but not contra-ception?*
- *If Catholics in this country ignore the Church's teaching and use contraception, why should anyone listen to what the Church says?*
- *If God created people as gay, why wouldn't he want them to have committed sexual relationships?*
- *If the Church regards gay people as "disordered," how can it oppose discrimination against them?*

Few issues are as neuralgic as homosexuality and contraception, which are considered here together because they concern the purpose and morality of sex. The idea that sex might have a purpose or meaning — a "good" — is nowadays countercultural: The common view is that if sex is consensual, it is legitimate. As the Archbishop of New York, Cardinal Timothy Dolan, put it in a January 2012 homily: "The one who, with God's grace and mercy, tries his or her best to be pure and chaste is often thought of not as a hero, not as a saint, but as a freak in our culture today."

Yet most people in their hearts know that sex is, or should be, more than pleasure-seeking between consenting adults, and should involve some degree of affection or commitment — or at least avoid making it a commodity. Most would agree that sex needs to have the right *context* in order to fulfill its purposes, which in turn presupposes boundaries. So it is not just the Church which believes in sexual morality, even if sometimes it seems that only the Church is prepared publicly to say what that morality should look like.

Elsewhere, there is widespread confusion about what moral constraints on sex should exist. The law draws boundaries, based on the principle of consent; but it seems arbitrary that in most U.S. states, an adult who has sex with a teenager whose sixteenth birthday falls on June 30 commits an illegal act on June 29 and a perfectly legal one on June 30.

The Church's view of sex is in keeping with the wisdom and insight of the ages, but not locked into the past. The Church holds that sex is essentially "good" if it occurs within a marriage between a man and a woman and is open to children; in this case, it conforms to God's design and is both procreative and unitive — that is, it deepens the bond between the man and the woman because it is open to new life. Outside that context, on the other hand, sex can be egotistical, destructive, and the cause of profound alienation between human beings.

Much has been written in Church documents since the Second Vatican Council, and especially in the teaching of Pope John Paul II known as *Theology of the Body*, about the power, beauty, and meaning of conjugal love. It is no longer true to say that either society or the Church regards the sole purpose of marriage to be children; its other essential purpose is "the good of the spouses," or conjugal love. There is nothing old-fashioned about the Catholic view of marriage: modern theology regards it as a vehicle for happiness and fulfilment. But there is also a radical, countercultural element of the Catholic view of marriage, which is that the two elements — the love of the spouses, and openness to children — are intertwined and should not be separated.

There are, therefore, two neuralgic elements in the question of sex and the Church. The first is the Church's teaching that sex belongs within marriage. The second is the Church's teaching that, within marriage, sex must be open to procreation. Both of these can be — and usually are — expressed negatively: the Church is against sex outside marriage, including homosexuality; and the Church is opposed to contraception, which severs the link between sex and children. Expressed positively, however, this teaching is an inspiring and uplifting one, and it is important that the reframing of this issue reflect the beauty of the Church's insights.

○3

POSITIVE INTENTION

The positive intention behind the criticism of the Church's teaching on homosexuality and contraception is the concern for people's welfare and dignity, and an awareness of the wrongness of scapegoating and condemnation. Contraception is seen as protecting people from the consequences of their actions — unplanned pregnancy — which could affect the lives of many. There is a concern that people are being harmed or sacrificed for the sake of dogmas and principles. We should have compassion for people who are not ready or willing to embrace conjugal love.

ଔ

The Meaning of Sex

Sex has a meaning, direction, and purpose. It can take us further away from or further toward the good for which it is intended. The degree of consent underpinning most modern views of sex ("as long as no one gets hurt") is insufficient. Just because it is consensual doesn't make it good, however much it may be sought or desired or freely engaged in, if it occurs outside the security and commitment of lifelong trust and intimacy between a husband and wife.

For proof that this is so, there is no shortage of evidence around us in the everyday experience of hurt and rejection. Who has not known, or does not know another who has known, the searing feeling of being treated as an object of desire, rather than an object of love? Love entails self-giving, surrender, a change in the way people focus their attention and energies onto another, and the security of a lifelong commitment. When sex happens without this change, a person is "lying" with their body, undermining something essential to the meaning of love. Sex can become simply an appetite with a tendency to treat persons as objects, which is why, perhaps, the modern experience of promiscuity is one of gratification followed quickly by boredom (people quickly tire of objects) and the feeling — by at least one of the parties — of being "used." Because this feeling is so common — almost universal — among those who have sex outside marriage, it suggests that sex does have a meaning or design or intrinsic purpose, a meaning which involves commitment, trust, and self-giving. The feeling of being "used" is usually accompanied by a horrible sense that we have given away too much of ourselves. One of the things we surrender in the act of love is knowledge about ourselves that we should give away only to someone to whom we have pledged, and who has pledged to us, lifelong love. As Cardinal Dolan put it in the same homily: "Truth be told, it is chastity and purity that liberates us, while immorality enslaves us."

We can have this discussion not needing to feel defensive. Judging by the misery in contemporary society, it is the modern permissive view of sexuality, rather than the Catholic view, which requires justification. That said, there is no doubt that the Church presents to our age a demanding understanding and ethic of marriage and sexuality, one that is often difficult to realize in practice and which even practicing Catholics either ignore or fall from; and this is particularly true in the case of contraception, where magisterial teaching is at least as often ignored as it is followed.

To critics it can seem that, if Church teaching is not accepted by Catholics, it is hardly likely to have any relevance to wider society. But this does not follow. Many Church teachings over the centuries have failed, in one generation or another, to convince the majority of the faithful. The Church has always taught the universal destination of material goods and the need to make responsible use of possessions (to "live simply," as the U.S. bishops say in *Faithful Citizenship*). Yet often Catholics have amassed large wealth with little or no concern for their neighbor. Or, to use another example, substantial numbers of American Catholics continue to advocate the death penalty for crimes such as murder, despite the clear opposition of the *Catechism*, popes, and the U.S. bishops.

Jesus' own followers frequently threw up their hands in despair at the apparent impossibility of obeying his teaching. The Church, Christ's instrument on earth, is frequently resented for making unrealistic demands on its followers. Yet attitudes change; the Church develops; the faithful learn. What one age regards as impossible and unrealistic another will see as normal and right, and vice versa. Sometimes the Church can be "out of touch" with the modern age because it is radically ahead of it — even of its own followers.

Birth Control

Church teaching is adamant that the deliberate decision to separate sex and fertility undermines the purpose and meaning of sex itself. The increasing use of contraception shows that sex and procreation are being pulled ever further apart.

In the 1983 *Code of Canon Law* marriage is described as a partnership (*consortium*) for the whole of life, which is ordered co-equally to two good ends: the good of the spouses (*bonum coniugum*) and the procreation and education of children (*bonum prolis*). The Second Vatican Council made clear that children are not the only purpose of marriage; conjugal love and children are equally important ends, indeed are vitally linked. The key document setting this out, Pope Paul VI's 1968 encyclical, *Humanae Vitae* ("Of Human Life"), refers to the "unitive" and the "procreative" elements of sex, and says they should not be separated.

Because the purpose of sex is conjugal love, and because one of the essential "ends" of marriage is children, contraception, which suppresses the capacity for procreation, is wrong, for it "closes the sexual act to the gift of life." Contraception deliberately makes the sexual act infertile by, for example, suppressing the production of eggs (the pill) or preventing the transmission of sperm (condoms). Contraception is described in *Humanae Vitae* as an action which, "whether in anticipation of the conjugal act, or in its accomplishment, or in the development of its natural consequences, proposes [*intendat*], whether as an end or as a means, to render procreation impossible" (no. 14, restated in the *Catechism,* no. 2370). In other words, contraception is not simply an action which impedes procreation, but an action impeding procreation carried out with an intent to do so. (As *Humanae Vitae* notes, using anti-ovulatory pills for medical reasons such as stemming excessive blood loss is not a form of contraception in the moral sense.)

But being opposed to contraception doesn't make Catholics "natalist" — in favor of enormous families. A married couple needs to "regulate" (in the *Catechism*'s words) the number of children they have, and it is "one of the aspects of responsible fatherhood and motherhood" to do so (see no. 2399). The question is how to do so in morally acceptable ways, respecting the meaning and purpose of sex rather than attempting to alter it.

Explaining why one is right and the other wrong is at the heart of what needs to be communicated on this point. This is not easy, because the Church's teaching starts from an assumption that is not widely shared — that sex has an intrinsic purpose (marriage that welcomes children), and that, for most people (including many Catholics), regulating births is synonymous with contraception.

Why Contraception Is Wrong but NFP Isn't

The Catholic Church has maintained the traditional Christian position, expressed in *Casti Connubi* (Pope Pius XI, 1931), that "since the conjugal act is destined primarily by nature for the begetting of children, those who in exercising it deliberately frustrate its natural power and purpose sin against nature." Pope Pius XII upheld this teaching and developed it, allowing for the use of the infertile period to regulate births. At the Second Vatican Council, the role which sex plays in marriage in deepening "conjugal love" between the husband and wife was stressed, along with the procreative element. This marked an important shift from a previous era in which marriage was seen primarily, or sometimes even exclusively, as an institution for the fostering of children and for social stability. The 1968 encyclical *Humanae Vitae* developed the links between the two aspects, unitive and procreative, noting that "to experience the gift of married love while respecting the laws of conception is to acknowledge that one is not the master of the sources of life but rather the minister of the design established by the Creator"(no. 13).

In canon law, consistent and constant use of contraception may demonstrate that an intention against children is "firm, intense, inflexible and non-negotiable" on the part of the couple, or one of them; in which case, it invalidates the marriage, because an essential property of marriage, the *bonum prolis*, has been excluded.

Otherwise, the Church encourages married couples to discern how many children it is responsible and right for them to have. "Let them thoughtfully take into account both their own welfare and that of their children, those already born and those which the future may bring," the Catholic bishops of the world declared in the Second Vatican Council document *Gaudium et Spes*. "For this accounting they need to reckon with both the material and the spiritual conditions of the times as well as of their state in life. Finally, they should consult the interests of the family group, of temporal society, and of the Church herself."

The modern method recommended by the Church for spacing children is known as natural family planning (NFP), of which there are a number of models or techniques. The spread and popularity of workshops and courses teaching these methods add up to a largely unreported "quiet revolution" in contemporary society, similar, in some ways, to the rise in new habits of ecological awareness such as recycling. Sadly, Catholics are almost as likely as everyone else to be ignorant of these techniques, which are at least as effective as contraceptive methods in enabling couples to plan births, yet unlike contraceptive methods, they do not suppress fertility.

Why is using this "natural" method of preventing conception acceptable, but not "artificial" methods? There are many good "organic" reasons, of which women are increasingly aware, of the damaging effects of the Pill and its side effects. Hormonal pills have a dampening effect on sexual libido. Many so-called contraceptives, such as the morning-after pill, are in fact abortafacients. And with "typical use," the failure rate of the Pill can be as high as 8 percent, because some women forget to take it every day. Modern women are turning against the Pill for many of the same reasons that they are turning against chemical-industrial food production or cosmetics.

But while there is much to be said about how much better (for people, for the planet) natural methods are, it is not because contraception is "artificial" that the Church rejects it (or it would need to deplore aspirin and other pills taken for headaches), but because, more importantly, contraception denies the purpose of the sexual act, and severs that act from its meaning. What is wrong is not the "unnaturalness" of the act, but the very attempt to have sex while simultaneously and intentionally trying to deprive it of its procreative purpose. Natural methods work with, and in conformity to, nature's own cycles, cycles which are designed to enable procreation only some of the time.

NFP and artificial contraception are very different: When used by couples to space children, sex using NFP is *non-procreative*, because it takes place during the infertile part of the woman's cycle; but artificial birth control enables sex that is *anti-procreative*. The couple using NFP is accepting their fertility as it is: a great good, but a good which they are not going to use at this time. The husband respects his wife's cycle and does not try to manipulate it or suppress it. Whereas a couple using artificial birth control treats their fertility as an inconvenience, a defect in need of improvement, or an illness, a couple using NFP recognizes fertility as a good and does nothing to deny this good.

They also produce different kinds of behavior. NFP requires self-mastery, a virtue developed through periodic abstinence; it strengthens the powers and the virtues of the human person, and makes it more likely that the sexual act is the product of a desire to express love for another, not the outcome of an ungovernable passion. As *Humanae Vitae* observes, such self-discipline "brings to family life abundant fruits of tranquillity and peace. It helps in solving difficulties of other kinds. It fosters in husband and wife thoughtfulness and loving consideration for one another. It helps them to repel inordinate self-love, which is the opposite of charity. It arouses in them a consciousness of their responsibilities. And finally, it confers upon parents a deeper and more effective influence in the education of their children" (no. 21).

The Church sees the powerful link between the proper use of sexuality, the strength of marriage, and the health of society. Key to all three is sexual self-discipline, which is necessary for deepening conjugal love. Contraception undermines that discipline; NFP builds it.

Homosexuality

"Sexuality has an intrinsic meaning and direction, which is not homosexual," says Pope Benedict XVI in *Light of the World*, because "evolution has brought forth sexuality for the purpose of reproducing the species." The idea that sex has an intrinsic purpose and meaning may seem strange to an age which regards it as the expression of intimacy or an act of pleasure. Yet however countercultural, what the Church teaches is quite in keeping with history and culture: the purpose and meaning of sex is to unite a man and a woman in order to give children a future. "This is the determination internal to the essence of sexuality," Pope Benedict adds. "Everything else is against sexuality's intrinsic meaning and direction."

The pope recognizes how unpopular this teaching is: "this is a point we need to hold firm," he says, "even if it is not pleasing to our age." The issue at stake here, he goes on, "is the intrinsic truth of sexuality's significance in the constitution of man's being."

The Church's teaching is sometimes described by critics as reflecting a visceral (homophobic) prejudice against gay people. Yet the *Catechism* has an objective and straightforward definition of homosexuality as referring to "relations between men or between women who experience an exclusive or predominant sexual attraction toward persons of the same sex" (no. 2357), and goes on to point out that this is nothing new. Homosexuality "has taken a great variety of forms through the centuries and in different cultures" says the *Catechism*, before adding that "its psychological genesis remains largely unexplained."

The Church, in other words, takes no position on the unresolved "nature versus nurture" debate about why some people are homosexually inclined, and therefore cannot be accused of homophobic ideas and language about gay people being in some way "unnatural."

Nor does the Church reject — as homophobes often do — the prevalence of the homosexual inclination: "the number of men and women who have deep-seated homosexual tendencies is *not negligible*" (no. 2358), says the *Catechism*, which is not something that homophobes would ever accept. The *Catechism* goes on to spend some paragraphs strongly opposing homophobia, using very strong language about the importance of accepting gay people with "respect, compassion and sensitivity," adding firmly that "every sign of unjust discrimination in their regard should be avoided."

Nothing in the Church's teaching on homosexuality justifies the accusation that it is contributing to the marginalization of, or prejudice against, gay people. It is also wrong to claim that the Church "is opposed to gay rights," although it is strongly opposed to some laws which have been advanced in the name of gay rights. The Church believes, for example, that marriage is a natural institution between a man and a woman; other kinds of union are not marriage. This is not an anti-gay-rights position, but a pro-marriage one.

Much of the modern "gay rights" agenda, in fact, has little to do with the original purpose of the movement to end prejudice and hostility against homosexual people in the law and in public opinion. But insofar as it adheres to that purpose, the Church supports it. In the 1980s, the Archbishop of Westminster in England, Cardinal Basil Hume, set down criteria for Catholics considering how to respond to proposed changes in the law claiming to eliminate discrimination or prejudice against gay people, but which may conceal other agendas or curb other rights. "Are there reasonable grounds for judging that the institution of marriage and the family could, and would, be undermined by a change in the law?" he asked. "Would society's rejection of a proposed change in the law be more harmful to the common good than the acceptance of such a change? Does a person's sexual orientation or activity constitute, in specific circumstances, a sufficient and relevant reason for treating that person in any way differently from other citizens?"

Cardinal Hume said these were "matters of practical judgment and assessment of social consequences, and thus must be considered case by case — and this without prejudice to Catholic teaching concerning homosexual acts."

Those last words are significant. Catholics are quite able to distinguish between the moral question of homosexuality — sex is reserved for marriage — and the civil rights of gay people, for the same reason they are able to discriminate between sins and crimes.

The Church believes that homosexual acts are immoral, yet favors their decriminalization. "With respect to the Church's position on a law that penalizes homosexuals or establishes the death penalty, there is nothing to discuss: She is absolutely opposed," said Vatican spokesman Father Federico Lombardi, S.J., at a Vatican press conference in 2008. "This is a position that respects the rights of the human person in his dignity." At the same time, he said, the Church "opposes the perspectives that lead some to say that sexual orientations should be placed on the same level in all situations and in relation to all norms" — and he went on to cite the question of marriage laws as one example.

The Church opposes all "unjust" discrimination against gay people while at the same time upholding the unique importance of marriage in law. Catholics can applaud and welcome the lifting of obstacles to the participation in civic life of gay people of recent years, while opposing attempts to enthrone an ideology which seeks to establish same-sex unions as equal in law to the marriage of a man and a woman, and what flows from this: same-sex adoption.

Just as the Church believes that a marriage between a man and a woman is in the best interests of society, it is also convinced that a child's best interests are served by being brought up by a man and a woman. In each case it is not that the Church "opposes gay rights," but rather that the Church favors the rights of children, and the duty of the state to protect marriage. So when the Church opposes attempts by the state to give special protection and rights to same-sex unions (or indeed to any sexual relations outside marriage) or same-sex adoption, it is not seeking to enforce prejudice against gay people; it is arguing that the good of society and children are best protected by reserving some legal privileges to marriage and restrictions on the right to adopt. There are many important rights at stake in this question — the common good of society, the rights of children — which trump the interests of particular groups.

Disorder, Sin, Inclination, Act

The language of some Vatican documents describing the homosexual orientation as "intrinsically disordered" has been misheard as describing gay people themselves. The word is a technical term from moral theology which can sound offensive in the light of the history of homophobic insults. But it is not part of that history; it is used simply to refer to an inclination away from the purpose and meaning of sex, which is conjugal love (married love open to children). In this sense many inclinations, not just homosexual ones, are "disordered." But "disordered" does not mean "sinful." What are sinful are homosexual *acts,* which the *Catechism* describes as "contrary to the natural law" because they "close the sexual act to the gift of life" and "do not proceed from a genuine affective and sexual complementarity."

All people, whatever their orientation, have a fundamental dignity and are loved by God. We are creatures of desire: some of those desires draw us closer to what is good (ennobling, liberating) for us; others lead us down blind alleys. These latter are "disordered" desires — including homosexual ones. But that doesn't make the desires *wrong* in themselves. It is the *actions* which flow from giving in to the desires that may be sinful. And those actions are not "inevitable" as some often claim: we are creatures of desire, but not its prisoners. We are not simply "driven" by our desires, sexual or otherwise, as if they were some kind of irresistible compulsion. Saying "no" to some desires is the beginning of morality. In its 1986 *Letter to the Bishops of the Catholic Church on the Pastoral Care of Homosexual Persons*, the Congregation for the Doctrine of the Faith said, "Although the particular inclination of the homosexual person is not a sin, it is a more or less strong tendency ordered toward an intrinsic moral evil; and thus the inclination itself must be seen as an objective disorder." It went on to say that it was "only in the marital relationship that the use of the sexual faculty can be morally good," and that therefore the one who *engages in homosexual behavior* is acting immorally.

It is not immoral or sinful, in other words, *to be gay*; what is sinful are *homosexual acts*. Explaining the CDF letter, Cardinal Hume's *Note on Church Teaching Concerning Homosexual People* observed that "the word 'disordered' is a harsh one in our English language. It immediately suggests a sinful situation or at least implies a demeaning of the person or even a sickness. It should not be so interpreted." He added that a homosexual orientation is "neither morally good nor morally bad; it is homosexual genital acts that are morally wrong."

Cardinal Hume went on: "When the Church speaks of the inclination to homosexuality as being 'an objective disorder' the Church can be thinking only of the inclination toward homosexual genital acts. The Church does not consider the whole personality and character of the individual to be thereby disordered. Homosexual people, as well as heterosexual people, can and often do give a fine example of friendship and the art of chaste loving."

The CDF letter notes: "To choose someone of the same sex for one's sexual activity is to annul the rich symbolism and meaning, not to mention the goals, of the Creator's sexual design. Homosexual activity is not a complementary union, able to transmit life, and so it thwarts the call to a life of that form of self-giving which the Gospel says is the essence of Christian living. This does not mean that homosexual persons are not often generous and giving of themselves; but when they engage in homosexual activity they confirm within themselves a disordered sexual inclination which is essentially self-indulgent."

The same letter earlier observes: "It is only in the marital relationship that the use of the sexual faculty can be morally good." Sex between a man and a woman, even in marriage, can also be egotistical and self-indulgent. But unlike the gay sexual act, the sexual act between man and woman is *ordered* to self-giving conjugal love, opening the couple to the generosity of accepting new life. (That may not be how the sexual act is in fact used; but that is what it is *ordered* to.)

The Church's Message to Gay People

It can sometimes seem as if the Church simply says "no" to gay people. What is heard is a series of prohibitions; but there is a more substantial part of the Church's message which often goes unheard.

The *Catechism* says gay people "are called to fulfill God's will in their lives and, if they are Christians, to unite to the sacrifice of the Lord's Cross the difficulties they may encounter from their condition" (no. 2358). The Church in this way recognizes that living a life of chastity can be a real challenge for a homosexual person, as indeed it is for all those who are not married, whatever their sexual inclination. It can be a call to love and generous self-giving but in a way that is different from the lifelong exclusivity of marriage.

It goes on: "By the virtues of self-mastery that teach them inner freedom, at times by the support of disinterested friendship, by prayer and sacramental grace, they can and should gradually and resolutely approach Christian perfection" (no. 2359).

Does that include finding love and fulfillment in a gay relationship? God gives every person the freedom and responsibility to decide how to live his or her life. He calls everyone to build loving relationships with other people, and to find fulfillment in genuine friendships. But it is only in marriage, in a lifelong commitment between a man and a woman, that intimacy should involve sex.

Sex is not a basic human need, like food or water; nor is it an essential means of growth and development, like family, community, or education. It is not a human right, and it is not a necessity. Many, many people, for many different reasons, do not get married, and live chaste lives. They are not less human, less happy, or less fulfilled as a result. They do not love less. Some of the richest, deepest, most fulfilling relationships of friendship are between people of the same sex.

It is a shame that this celibate love, if it is directed toward another of the same gender, is now assumed to be homosexual — conditioned by homoerotic attraction, even if not acted upon. Society is losing the vocabulary to speak about intense friendships between people of the same sex. This makes discussion of this topic hard.

There are many different ways of loving and forming friendships. But sex has a very particular meaning — to bind a husband and wife together and open their love to the gift of new life. This is the *meaning* of sex. Gay sex is not just an alternative expression of love to heterosexual sex; it is an expression of sexual love that has something missing — namely, the possibility of giving new life, and the complementarity of the love between a man and woman. Without that complementarity and openness to life, sex lacks its true purpose.

☙

Existing Frame

"The Church is obsessed with sexuality, whether heterosexual or gay. If God made people gay, isn't it terrible to condemn them to a life

of celibacy? And why does the Church call gay people disordered? The Church's views on contraception are outdated, and it's clear that many practicing Catholics, particularly in the West, simply ignore this teaching."

REFRAME

Sexual morality is all about developing our capacity for self-giving love so that we don't use others. The proper context for sex is a lifelong commitment between husband and wife. The Church welcomes and embraces gay people. Many committed Catholics are gay, living faithful and chaste lives. You'll find homosexual people at Mass and working for the Church. The Church rejects discrimination and prejudice against homosexual people. Church teaching does not say homosexual people are disordered, but that sex is ordered to marriage and children, and that is why homosexual people, like all of us who are unmarried, are called to chastity as the best way of learning self-giving love. Of course, marriage may be closed to homosexual people, as it is to many people. But like everyone else who is not married or cannot marry, homosexual people are called to develop intimate, trusting, loving (but chaste) relationships.

Key Messages

- Natural family planning in its modern form is a means of using a woman's fertility to enable people to plan their families. It is highly effective, both for conceiving children, and for spacing them. It involves a couple cooperating; it involves a shared responsibility. It's natural, organic, and respects the body and its cycles, rather than suppressing them.
- Catholics are against artificial contraception because it suppresses fertility rather than regulates it. Not every sexual act will be fertile, but you shouldn't separate sex from its meaning, which is for creating new life and for deepening committed love.
- The "contraceptive culture" proposes suppresing fertility, and leads to the notion that sex is about recreation, not procreation and commitment.
- Sex should be open to children. That is the meaning of it. Sex is a blessing. It is a call to love. But it must be framed within commitment and stability, otherwise the body is lying.

- We favor laws which outlaw discrimination against homo-sexual people, but not laws which undermine the special place of marriage or which are against the best interests of a child. Cohabiting couples may need protection and support in law with regard to inheritance, tax, and other financial issues, but marriage, which can be only between a man and a woman, is a unique institution which deserves special protection, and is the proper place for a child.
- The Church does not oppose same-sex marriage and adoption because it is against equality or gay rights, but rather because other interests and rights (especially those of the child) should weigh more heavily in the balance.

Chapter 3

EQUALITY AND RELIGIOUS FREEDOM

— Challenging Questions —

- *Why should the Church be allowed to discriminate against gay people when the law forbids it?*
- *If Catholic adoption agencies don't want to obey the law, why should they then have access to public funds?*
- *Why should the Church be allowed to impose its narrow view of the family through taxpayer-funded services?*

Laws banning discrimination against minorities — especially in recent years against gay people — have led, in many Western countries, to arguments between the Church and state. Catholics are accused of being "opposed to equality," of "seeking the right to discriminate," and failing to grasp a basic tenet of liberal democracy— namely, the equality of every individual before the law.

Some of the criticism is prejudiced, raising old ghosts of Catholics as having "dual loyalties," or of trying to "impose" the Church's view. Some is particularly fierce, especially from gay-rights lobbies who see the Church as the enemy of what they see as one of the great successes of the modern era: the emancipation of gay people.

The framing of this issue — of a reactionary Church opposing equality — is tragic, given that the ideal of equality is rooted in the basic Christian principle that all are equal in worth and dignity before God. It is also inaccurate in that it supposes that "equality" is a fixed notion, something people either believe in or not. In fact it is a strongly contested notion because it raises questions of values and rights. As Aristotle said, "The worst form of inequality is to try to make unequal things equal." Not every difference reflected in the law is discrimination; and equality should not mean equivalence.

The Church talks about *unjust* discrimination — something it is firmly against. A "just" or "legitimate" discrimination is when the law

refuses to recognizes an equal right for good reasons. Thus the law prohibits racially segregated public restrooms, but not public restrooms segregated by gender. The first is discriminatory, but not the second. In the
first case, the motivation is irrational prejudice (there can be no other
reason for racially dividing restrooms); in the second the motive is the
recognition of legitimately differing needs and rights: it is "reasonable,"
and not discriminatory, for men to be excluded from women's restrooms
and vice versa, because there are legitimate needs being met by such
discrimination.

So not everything that someone might regard as "discrimination"
would the Church agree to be so. The Church does not believe, for
example, in the "right of gay people to marry," because it believes that
marriage is designed for a man and a woman for the sake of children.
"Discrimination" in modern Western societies is a "boo" word, a term
that can quite irrationally unite people against a perceived scandal. The
Church is accused, for example, of asking for the "freedom to discriminate against gay people" when it says it should be legal for its adoption
agencies to place children only with married couples. But this is an
absurdly unjust frame. "Discrimination" means separating or excluding
for irrational, prejudiced, or unfounded reasons. Where the exclusion is
reasonable, or the result of weighing other rights in the balance — in this
case, the right of children to a mother and father — t is not discrimination. It is reasonable to distinguish in law between the natural institution
of marriage, entered into by a man and a woman in part for procreation,
and other forms of union, which are not "equal" (in that they do not
serve the same social good) and therefore do not call for the same protection and encouragement by the law.

So the argument over equality needs to start by reminding people
of the purpose of the "equality" project. It is not (or should not be) an
attempt to give everything and everybody an equivalent legal status, but
a drive to remove unjust barriers to participation in society, democracy,
and the economy. Discrimination occurs when things or people that
should be treated in the same way by the law are treated less favorably.
But when that differential is reasonable or just, it is not discrimination.
Ultimately, therefore, we cannot avoid a debate about whether things or
people do or do not have an equal value — whether, say, the biological
union of a man and a woman should have equal value (in the law) to a
same-sex union.

The other neuralgic issue in this area concerns the way equality laws are implemented. Giving "equality" to one group in society can seriously prejudice the rights and interests of another group. The Church is a passionate advocate of the general principle of curbing discrimination — that no one should be allowed in law to refuse to employ or offer a service to someone on the grounds of race, gender, or disability. The disagreements arise over *how* those equality laws are implemented. And behind that clash are different perceptions of a liberal and pluralistic society.

Sometimes laws are proposed or enacted which directly affect the Church's "natural" freedoms and rights, or which seek to coerce Catholics in a way that violates their conscience. This goes against the principle, dating back to the founding of the United States, that the law should be applied wherever possible in such a way that accommodates minorities. In 1789, shortly after becoming the first U.S. president, George Washington wrote to a group of Quakers who were concerned they would be required to perform military service in violation of their conscience and religious belief in order to assure them "very explicitly that in my opinion the conscientious scruples of all men should be treated with great delicacy and tenderness; and it is my wish and desire that the laws may always be as extensively accommodated to them as a due regard to the protection and essential interests of the nation may justify and permit."

Military conscientious objection is a classic example of the accommodation of minorities on the basis of conscience. Another is the long tradition of allowing court witnesses or newly elected politicians who are non-Christian, or object to oath-making, instead to make a solemn "affirmation" without putting a hand on the Bible. In more recent decades, "conscience clauses" at the national level and in a number of states protect doctors, pharmacists, and other health practitioners from providing services or drugs to which they object as a matter of conscience.

Catholics strongly disagreed with the 1973 Supreme Court decision *Roe v. Wade* legalizing abortion, and have continued to argue against it. The law respects that disagreement. Federal laws and regulations prohibit hospitals and other institutions receiving public funds from requiring doctors and nurses to participate in abortions.

The law, in other words, balances the law's position that a woman is free to choose an abortion with the recognition that a Catholic is free in conscience not to have to carry one out. The law is the law; and all are equal before it. But it is *applied differently* to different groups. This is an essential principle in the equalities project. Minorities need, sometimes, to be protected from the effect of a law. They are not being allowed to "opt out" of the law. They remain fully subject to it, but the law treats them differently.

Allowing such exemptions is crucial to a healthy coexistence in a pluralistic society. It is also necessary in a democracy which allows the freedom of faith alongside the freedom of other faiths or secular beliefs. Disagreements between Church and state over this issue does not indicate a reactionary Church in conflict with a liberal state — the usual frame. They are really about two models of a liberal society, in which the Church's model has the stronger liberal credentials, reflecting a deeper, richer pluralism, as opposed to a narrower, individualist model of liberal democracy.

Modern democracies separate church and state in the sense that states are not "confessional." Modern states do not seek to impose Christian beliefs on people, as happens in theocracies. But nor should they be "secular theocracies," coercing Christians into acting against their consciences by imposing beliefs contrary to those convictions. As a rule, the state should reflect the variety of beliefs in society and seek to enact laws which are sensitive to the needs and rights of those diverse groups.

This is an example of what Pope Benedict XVI has referred to as a "positive secularity" — namely, a religiously and ideologically neutral state which nevertheless respects and understands the needs and rights of faith. What the Church objects to as undemocratic is what Pope Benedict XVI calls "aggressive secularism," in which the state fails to recognize the natural freedoms and rights of the Church in the public square, reducing religion to a merely private matter, in which the Church is treated as an association of like-minded individuals rather than, as should be the case, a "natural society" with its intrinsic freedoms and rights.

At the heart of this issue, then, is a question of weighing two essential freedoms: equality (or "freedom from discrimination") with freedom of religion. A law which exaggerates one freedom at the expense of the other is a bad law.

What is freedom of religion? A key element of it is that charities and religious bodies should be free to "manifest belief" — namely, to create organizations inspired by and witnessing to their religious ethos. That means selecting certain kinds of people to run them, and having policies and practices which witness to the values underpinning them. Faith-based organizations must be free to be consistent with their beliefs by the way they act, as long as they do not offend public order or inhibit the rights and freedoms of others. This freedom is much larger and more contentious than the "freedom of worship." It is also vital to civil society, which is nurtured and sustained by such value-driven organizations.

Neither equality nor religious freedom is limitless. Equality is not an absolute; nor is religious freedom. The common good of society calls for limits on both. But the common good also calls them to be kept in balance. That has become harder in recent years because of the prevalence of a secular liberal mentality which sees only individuals, not the organizations and associations which connect them. The belief that rights are essentially assertions of individual autonomies has led governments to exaggerate the first (equality) while failing to grasp the significance of the second (religious freedom).

CB

POSITIVE INTENTION

The positive intention in this argument is underpinned by the belief that in a modern pluralistic society we should all be equal before the law and have equal rights regardless of race, religion, gender, sexual orientation, or disability. Legislation has rightly been put in place to ensure this. So it seems clearly right and just, for example, that a wheelchair user should have as equal access as an able-bodied person to public buildings. Or that a woman cannot be fired from her job simply because she is pregnant. Or that a white candidate should not be preferred to a black candidate during a job interview simply on grounds of race. The positive intention behind the criticism of the Church's opposition to, say, same-sex adoption appeals to the core Christian principle of the equal dignity and worth of every human being, and the historic Gospel task of emancipating those who have been marginalized and excluded.

CB

The Civil-Society Principle

Religious freedom is not a small matter for the Church — or for society as a whole. As one of the leading actors in civil society — running a large network of schools, hospitals, charities, and so on — it understands the importance of religious motivation. People set up, work for, and give their lives to church organizations because their faith inspires them. Feeling grateful for the gifts of God, being people of compassion and sensitive to the needs of the world, and often fired by a strong sense of social justice and civic commitment, they establish schools, homeless shelters, child-welfare charities, adoption agencies, hospices, and countless other projects and institutes tackling addiction, family breakdown, and poverty in all its forms. As we saw in the last chapter, the Catholic Church is a remarkable contributor to the common good in this respect.

Nor are these Catholic organizations at the service only of other Catholics: they serve the whole of society, addressing the needs of people whatever their beliefs or backgrounds. The result is that Catholic civil organizations make a massive contribution to the common good of the United States, worth many tens of billions of dollars. That is why the "freedom to manifest belief" is so essential to a healthy civil society. Without the freedom to witness to the values of the Gospel and the teachings of the Catholic Church — what is usually described as a "Catholic ethos" — these organizations would shrivel and die, or become empty shells, to the detriment of all. You can't have the fruits without the roots.

Catholics are called to help people in need, whatever their religion. Most citizens know enough about Jesus and his works to recognize that his followers' caring ministries deserve respect, even (or especially) when they benefit not just Catholics but the health and human services of the entire nation. Sister Mary Ann Walsh, R.S.M., the director of media relations for the United States Conference of Catholic Bishops, puts it this way: "The goal is to help people in need because they are fellow children of God, whether or not they pray beside you on Sunday."

Laws which seek to free people from discrimination — in themselves a worthy objective applauded by the Church — must take care that they don't restrict the freedom to manifest belief which is vital to the flourishing of these organizations. It is wrong, in principle, for an actively homosexual person (in a civil partnership, say) to be denied a job simply on the grounds of that orientation, where that orientation is not remotely relevant to the job — as an accountant, for example. But if that person applies to be the principal of a Catholic school, it *is* relevant, because the Church teaches that active homosexuality is wrong, and the principal of a Catholic school is responsible for witnessing to, and upholding, the ethos of the school.

An anti-discrimination law which made it illegal for a school to "discriminate" in this way would quickly undermine its ethos, and therefore its reason for existing. This is recognized in U.S. law (above all, Title VII of the Civil Rights Act of 1964). In a January 11, 2012, judgment, the Supreme Court upheld the principle of "ministerial exception" to anti-discrimination laws, referring to a specific exemption that applies to those who represent the beliefs of a religious organization. "Requiring a church to accept or retain an unwanted minister, or punishing a church for failing to do so, intrudes upon more than a mere employment decision," the judges said. "Such action interferes with the internal governance of the church, depriving the church of control over the selection of those who will personify its beliefs. By imposing an unwanted minister, the state infringes the Free Exercise Clause, which protects a religious group's right to shape its own faith and mission through its appointments."

Do such exemptions adversely affect others? No, because people have a choice about which school they apply to be a teacher in; or they can choose between different suppliers of particular goods and services. If the only schools were Catholic schools, of course, it would be a different matter, but there are many more non-Catholic schools than Catholic ones.

It is also important, of course, for the "discrimination" in these cases to be reasonable, or what the Church would call "just." A woman responsible for cleaning the classrooms does not need to be a Catholic, or leading a lifestyle consistent with a Catholic ethos, because her job does not involve *per se* setting an example or witnessing; the ministerial exemption does not apply. In the same way, respect for religious freedom does not mean accommodating any preference dressed up as conviction, or which a religious group claims to be religious.

The delicate balancing act required in law has often gone wrong in recent years as laws are enacted which fail to recognize the importance of the freedom of religion. Because of the growing secularization of the governing classes — a lack of empathy or understanding among some politicians for what makes faith organizations tick — there have been clashes with the Church. The U.S. bishops felt compelled in 2011 to create a special Committee on Religious Liberty to address the problem.

Testifying before a House subcommittee on October 26, 2011, the committee's chairman, Bishop William E. Lori of Bridgeport, Connecticut, recalled the long tradition of religious freedom in America and its pre-eminent place in the Bill of Rights. "The bishops of the United States have watched with increasing alarm as this great national legacy of religious liberty, so profoundly in harmony with our own teachings, has been subject to ever more frequent assault and ever more rapid erosion," he warned, and cited five federal examples:

- The U.S. Department of Health and Human Services' decision in August 2011 to mandate coverage of contraception (including those causing chemical abortions) and sterilization as "preventive services" in almost all private health insurance plans, as part of implementation of the 2010 Patient Protection and Affordable Care Act. Bishop Lori, borrowing a phrase from the president of the Catholic Health Association, said the regulations' exemption for religious employers "is so incredibly narrow that it would cover only the 'parish housekeeper'" and "does nothing to protect insurers or individuals with religious or moral objections to the mandate." Bishop Robert Lynch of St. Petersburg, Florida, announced he would be forced to end the health insurance plan for the diocese's 2,300 employees unless a stronger exemption were crafted. The irony is that the bishops were some of the strongest supporters of the Affordable Care Act's goal of extending health care coverage to millions of uninsured Americans, but throughout the legislative process criticized the bill's lack of conscience protections.
- The U.S. Department of Health and Human Services's decision in May 2011 to require the full range of reproductive services — including abortion and contraception — from agencies contracting with the government to provide services to human trafficking victims and unaccompanied minor refugees. "Already," Bishop Lori noted, "HHS has taken its major program for serving trafficking victims away from [the bishops' highly rated Migrants and

Refugees Services] and transferred it to several smaller organizations that frankly may not be equipped to assume this burden."

- "The State Department's U.S. Agency for International Development (USAID) is increasingly requiring contractors, such as Catholic Relief Services (CRS), to provide comprehensive HIV-prevention activities (including condom distribution), as well as full integration of its programs with reproductive health activities (including provision of artificial contraception) in a range of international relief and development programs."

- The Department of Justice filed a brief in July 2011 in a U.S. District court siding with a lesbian federal employee's challenge of the Defense of Marriage Act, after announcing months earlier it considered DOMA unconstitutional. The brief says the rationale for the Act can be understood only as "hostility" toward homosexuals. "If the label of 'bigot,'" Bishop Lori said, "sticks to our Church and many other churches — especially in court, under the Constitution — because of their teaching on marriage, the result will be church-state conflicts for many years to come."

- Turning to the state level, Bishop Lori said religious liberty protections, particularly with regard to laws redefining marriage to include same-sex couples, "have fallen far short of what is necessary." He noted that after New York's passage of same-sex marriage, at least one county clerk is being sued for refusing to sign same-sex marriage certificates (she arranged for a delegate instead) "and gay-rights advocates boast how little religious-freedom protection individuals and groups will enjoy under the new law."

The Adoption Agencies: A Case in Point

Catholic adoption agencies, affiliated with Catholic Charities USA, arrange nearly a third of the 136,000 adoptions that take place in the United States annually. But in a growing number of jurisdictions — Massachusetts, Washington, D.C., and, in 2011, Illinois — they have been forced out of that social service because they won't place children with same-sex couples (just as they won't with cohabiting couples or singles).

For a Catholic agency, opening up adoption service to same-sex couples is unthinkable. The Church has made some strong comments in the past about same-sex adoption. It considers same-sex adoption as not in a child's best interests because it denies them the gift of a mother and father who would take the place of their own natural parents. Marriage, and the love of a mother and father, are the best forms of family life for a growing child.

Proving this is not always easy. The psychological impact of same-sex adoption on children remains hotly debated by psychologists, and the best that can be said is that the jury is still out on the matter.

What is not in doubt are the statistics on stability. Children born into married unions are twice as likely as those born to cohabiting couples to spend their childhoods with their natural parents; the figures for cohabiting same-sex couples are even worse than those for cohabiting heterosexual couples, fewer than one in ten of whom are still together after ten years. Nor is there much doubt that same-sex adoption reduces the number of relationship role models, depriving a child of the male/ female relationship, a mother and father coordinating parenting, and either a father-child or a mother-child relationship.

But the issue is not solely, or even mainly, about whether same-sex parents offer as good an environment for children as other kinds of parents. It is about the freedom of an adoption agency to decide that question for themselves. There is a key freedom at stake: the freedom to take a stand in promoting the value and importance of marriage, which is no longer the bedrock of society. This is a good example of a Catholic ethos — to be a sign of contradiction in modern society, to point to values which are being eroded or undermined. For Catholic adoption agencies, it is key to their reason for existing.

The Illinois Catholic Charities adoption agencies were shut down through implementation of a November 2010 law ironically named "The Illinois Religious Freedom Protection and Civil Unions Act." The law does nothing to protect religious freedom; its purpose is to grant couples, including same-sex couples, the right to form civil unions and thereby enjoy the same benefits as married couples. Months after it was signed into law, the Illinois Department of Children and Family Services informed the Catholic agencies that they would have to consider same-sex couple applicants if they wanted to continue to receive state funds. One closed immediately. A few others banded together to raise a legal challenge but were forced to abandon it when a court refused to allow them to continue operating during the appeals process.

"In the name of tolerance, we're not being tolerated," Bishop Thomas J. Paprocki of the Diocese of Springfield, Illinois, a civil and canon lawyer, told *The New York Times*.

Some of the agencies having been working with orphaned children for more than a century, and in modern times accounted for 20 percent of the state's adoptions. A crucial witness — as well as a vital service to Illinois society — was lost.

The Dictatorship of Relativism

Some argue that if a law prohibits discrimination one cannot have exceptions to that law on principle. Yet anti-discrimination laws have often been enacted, as shown above, with exemptions for charities and faith-based organizations. Others argue that the agencies were in receipt of public funds, and that the condition for public funding was that a service had to be equally open to all. But again, there are many instances — faith-based charities, for example — where that principle has never been applied, because the other "good" involved (preserving the ethos) counterbalances it. "It's true that the Church doesn't have a First Amendment right to have a government contract," says Anthony R. Picarello Jr., general counsel and associate general secretary of the U.S. bishops' conference, "but it does have a First Amendment right not to be excluded from a contract based on its religious beliefs."

Some appeal to the example of anti-racist or gender-equality laws achieving over time the eradication of racist or sexist attitudes. Should the law allow an agency to refuse a black couple, by appealing to some passage of Scripture? But that comparison was odious. That would be an example of "unjust" discrimination, of irrational prejudice rather than reasonable conviction.

The justification for refusing the exemption essentially comes down to a view which alarms the bishops: that the Church was "homophobic" and that the law was a means of forcing the Church either to adopt a more "progressive" attitude or pay the price. It was a means, in other words, of using the law to coerce the Church into altering its teaching, in much the same way as the law might be used to coerce people into renouncing racist or antisocial behavior.

Yet to refuse a same-sex couple the right to adopt was not irrational prejudice; it arises from a deep-seated conviction about the nature of the family which has long been the bedrock of human society. Many nowadays disagree that the "traditional family" is in any way preferable to alternatives (same-sex, single-parent, etc.), but is the state really now declaring that it is "irrational prejudice" to believe otherwise?

Behind the refusal to grant exemptions for Catholic charities is the idea that the state acts on society in order to condition it, to impose a certain ideological view, in this case, of the family. It also implies a model of society in which there is no such thing as "intermediate associations," only individuals, families, and the state. In the traditional Christian understanding, people do not belong just to families, but have other, wider allegiances — to communities of value, with different moral narratives. A nation, in this vision, is a "community of communities." It is the state's task to regulate the relationships between these communities, to prevent them from accumulating powers which prevent other communities from flourishing; it is not the state's task to impose an ideological narrative. But in the individualist liberal conception of state and society, there is nothing but a state and many individuals; therefore, one moral narrative — in this case, that same-sex couples are equal to traditional couples — must prevail.

In the case of adoption agencies, government is telling the Church that its organizations must accept the principle that same-sex couples are equal to the traditional family, and that this principle trumps their freedom to continue to advocate otherwise. This is what Pope Benedict memorably called the "dictatorship of relativism," which is as illiberal as the theocratic principle that the only form of union recognized by the state is Christian marriage. Ironically, therefore, the Church — often accused of opposing liberal values — has become sometimes a lonely advocate of a core liberal principle.

Against this is an ideological view of the state, which contradicts a key element of the Catholic understanding of the public square. It is not the state's task to condition the consciences of its people, but to regulate and balance different rights and freedoms. This argument is not about the freedom of religious organizations to "discriminate," but about whether the state should be allowed to interfere with religious organizations and to impose on them relativist ideologies. Through such laws the government tells civil-society organizations that if they wish to exist, and receive public funding, they must adhere to an ideological view that same-sex families are just as good for children and for society as the traditional family. That message sends a chill down the spines of the leaders not just of the Catholic Church but of other churches and faith organizations.

In a January 12, 2012, letter religious leaders in the United States warned that redefining marriage would result in faith organizations being pressured into treating same-sex sexual conduct as the moral equivalent of marital sexual conduct, leading to many church-state conflicts. Even when religious groups succeeded in avoiding civil liability, "they would face other government sanctions — the targeted withdrawal of government cooperation, grants, or other benefits." After giving a number of recent examples of this, the religious leaders, including a number of Catholic bishops, warned that "the refusal of these religious organizations to treat a same-sex sexual relationship as if it were a marriage marked them and their members as bigots, subjecting them to the full arsenal of government punishments and pressures reserved for racists."

In 2011, the Pontifical Academy of Social Sciences, headed by American law professor Mary Ann Glendon, held its plenary session on the question of religious liberty and threats to it around the world today. The critique was not all aimed at such tightly controlled regimes as Iran and North Korea. In her summary speech, Glendon said: "Even in countries where religious liberty has a long and apparently secure constitutional foundation, the suspicion of those religious believers who claim to know truths about the human person leads to marginalization and even outright discrimination. Many democratic states harbor within them totalitarian impulses which threaten religious liberty."

She went on to quote Pope Benedict's message to the assembly, which could be read as a reminder to those in Western democracies not to take religious freedom for granted. Freedom, she quoted, is "a challenge held out to each generation, and it must constantly be won over for the cause of good."

CS

EXISTING FRAME

"The Catholic Church, like other Christian bodies, has a retrograde, homophobic, and irrational view of homosexuality which is out of step with progressive, liberal values of tolerance. It uses its power and resources to lobby the government to be allowed to disobey the law in order to

continue to promote its homophobia. All organizations should operate within the law, and no organization, particularly one in receipt of public money, should be allowed to continue to promote its divisive, intolerant views or to continue to discriminate against the gay minority."

Reframe

The Catholic Church is one of the world's leading advocates of equality and human rights, and believes nobody should be subject to unjust discrimination. This issue is not about the right to discriminate, but about the balance of freedoms in a modern pluralistic society — the need for some groups to be free from discrimination, and the freedom to form organizations and witness to their beliefs. It is about how equality laws are framed in such a way that reflects that balance. The Church is not asking to be exempt from the law; it is asking for the law to be implemented differently for different groups, as happens already in many laws, in order to preserve a greater good. A healthy civil society hinges on the freedom of faith-based and other organizations with strong values to create and run those organizations in accordance with those values, as long as they don't inhibit other people's freedoms.

ଓଃ

Key Messages

- The modern principle of equality has its roots in the Christian principle that all people are of equal value; this principle underlies the abolition of the slave trade and the civil-rights movements of the 1950s and 1960s. The Catholic Church is globally one of the leading advocates of equality and rights — for the elderly, the unborn, immigrants, women, and gay people. The Church does not oppose equality, but finds itself opposed to the way equality laws are sometimes implemented in the modern era in ways that negatively affect other rights and freedoms.
- Protecting minorities from unjust discrimination is one of the major tasks of the modern state. They remain fully subject to the law, but the law treats them differently.
- When the Church asks for exemptions, it is not trying to condition the law in accordance with its beliefs ("imposing its views") but appealing to a well-established principle in mod-

ern democracy and European rights law — the need to protect, in law, the freedom to associate and to manifest belief, which is the key principle underlying the U.S. Constitution. The corollary of a vigorous civil society is religious freedom.

- The Church's advocacy of marriage as an institution deserving of protection by the state stems from the unique nature of marriage as beneficial to children and for society in general. Excluding from it those who do not meet its essential conditions is not discrimination but an attempt to preserve its unique nature.

Chapter 4

ASSISTED SUICIDE

— Challenging Questions —

- *Why does the Church oppose allowing people to choose the time of their own death?*
- *If a person of sound mind who is terminally ill and in dreadful pain wishes to die, why should the law prevent them by prosecuting those who assist them?*
- *Doctors have always helped people on their way to death; how is legal assisted suicide any different?*
- *What right does the Church have to tell people of no faith how they should end their lives?*
- *Society is changing its mind about assisted dying, as opinion polls show. Isn't this another case of the Church trying to legislate for everyone else?*

The drive to make it legal to help someone commit suicide is one of the principal — perhaps *the* principal — ethical debates of our time, comparable, in its way, to the debate over legalizing abortion in the 1960s. The U.S. Supreme Court ruled in 1997 that states could prohibit physician-assisted suicide; there is no constitutional right, therefore, to ask a doctor to administer drugs that cause death. But physician-assisted suicide is legal in Oregon, Washington, and Montana, and pressure is mounting in other states, too.

The case in favor is at heart one of personal autonomy: If a person is suffering unbearably, and wishes to end their life at a particular point, and in the manner of their choosing, who has any right to decide for them?

But the question is not about the legality of suicide, which is no longer a formal crime in any state (nor is it a right) but about the legality of bringing about another's suicide, which raises a large number of other issues.

The campaign to allow assisted suicide arises in part from modern advances in medical technology, but also from a society which has lost sight of the meaning of suffering. An aging population means a greater prevalence of long-term, terminal conditions such as motor neurone disease, Parkinson's, and Alzheimer's, which bring about great changes in a person and undoubted suffering. A man or woman nowadays faces years of debilitating illness and suffering in a way that would be unknown in previous eras.

Such conditions often mean the loss of capacities and abilities which a person has relied on. A high-profile campaigner for an assisted-suicide law in the United Kingdom, the best-selling novelist Terry Pratchett, fears the day that his Alzheimer's will mean he can no longer write. That moment, he said in a TV documentary in June 2011, would mean for him "the end" — one he would rather avoid by swallowing barbiturates. Such feelings are understandable, and common. In a high-achieving society, people build their egos and satisfaction around their successes and powers. But are lives less worth living once these vanish? Whatever an individual may conclude, are we as a society prepared to endorse that idea? And what effect would that have on the way society views the elderly, or indeed the poor, the disabled, and the unsuccessful?

Until the 1960s, assisted suicide, or "voluntary euthanasia," as it was then known, was one of the options advanced by the eugenics movement to help rid society of "undesirables." "The moment we face it frankly we are driven to the conclusion that the community has a right to put a price on the right to live in it," wrote the playwright and eugenicist George Bernard Shaw in 1934. "If people are fit to live, let them live under decent human conditions. If they are not fit to live, kill them in a decent human way."

Advocates of legalizing euthanasia reject the comparison with the eugenicists of the 1920s and 1930s who paved the way for the Nazi death camps; where eugenicists favored *compulsory* sterilization, abortion, and euthanasia, the modern case for assisted dying rests, like that of abortion, on the "right to choose." It has become a question of autonomy. It is for the sovereign individual to determine, coolly and with forethought, the manner and time of his death. As Pratchett put it in a speech in February 2010: "It seems to me quite a reasonable and sensible decision for someone with a serious, incurable, and debilitating disease to elect for a medically assisted death by appointment."

Yet in both cases — the eugenicist call for euthanasia and the modern call for assisted suicide — a judgment is being made about the lack of worth of a human life. It may seem amazing now to recall that between 1915 and 1919 a Chicago surgeon, Harry Haiselden, publicly allowed six infants he diagnosed as hereditarily unfit to die by withholding treatment, and went on to make a movie, *Black Stork*, about a doctor who did the same (it was still being shown in American cinemas in the 1940s). But in the case of an assisted suicide, a depressed or sick person is making the same decision about themselves. They have internalized the message that their life is not worth preserving.

Such a choice may seem to that individual "reasonable," but it is not reasonable or desirable for the law to sanction such a choice. As with abortion, the argument turns on the extent to which personal autonomy should trump other considerations. In the case of assisted suicide, no one else's life is being taken, which makes the personal-autonomy case appear more compelling. Yet it is a fallacy to suppose that in a decision like this that decision can ever be "individual." Suicide has a profound impact on others. Our lives are interconnected in countless ways. Allowing for the exercise of autonomy in this case would rapidly alter the conditions for others in society.

ଔ

Positive Intention

There are many positive values in the case for legalizing assisted suicide. It is compassionate to seek to help someone suffering serious pain to be free of it. Some people view their lives as so altered by suffering that what they endure obliterates everything else. The only possible response to such stories is compassion and sympathy. There is a positive intention, too, behind those who point to the many failings in the way the dying are treated in hospitals, sometimes with inadequate pain relief, or poorly cared for. The experience of seeing someone you love endure inadequate care can produce a horror of dying.

ଔ

Why the Church Opposes Euthanasia

In common with a long-standing tradition of Western civilization, the Church believes that dying naturally is a vital part of life's journey, in many ways the most meaningful part. Dying can be described as a process of healing. Important things happen on that journey, and suffering and pain are often a part of it. As Cardinal Daniel N. DiNardo of Galveston-Houston, chairman of the U.S. Conference of Catholic Bishops' Committee on Pro-Life Activities, said at the June 2011 release of the U.S. bishops' first comprehensive policy statement on assisted suicide: "Compassion isn't to say, 'Here's a pill.' It's to show people the ways we can assist you, up until the time the Lord calls you."

Dying, then, is a highly meaningful gradual process of renunciation and surrender. Although some die swiftly and painlessly, very often the pattern of dying involves great suffering, because (and this is true of old age in general) it involves letting go of those things which in our lives we believe make us worthwhile and lovable: our looks, intelligence, abilities, and capabilities. This is what the great Swiss psychiatrist Carl Jung called "necessary suffering," the suffering endured by the ego, which protests at having to change and surrender. The idea that this kind of suffering is part of growth is not a uniquely "religious" view, although Christianity — with the Cross and the Resurrection at its heart — has perhaps a richer theological understanding than most secular outlooks.

Yet while the Church urges the need to accept necessary suffering, it works to relieve and avoid what might be called "unnecessary suffering." The abandonment and renunciation of illness and dying require loving support and sophisticated palliative care. Excessive physical pain, and the loneliness of abandonment, can and should be avoided.

That is why it is church organizations, pioneered in the United Kingdom and the United States in the 1950s by the hospice movement, have transformed the way society now cares for the dying. "Last days are not . . . lost days," declared Cicely Saunders, the British founder of many hospices. Rather than seeing themselves as burdensome and unwanted, she believed that people with terminal illness should be in circles of love and care where they will be valued and made comfortable.

Hospices meet the needs of the dying much better than hospitals, which are not geared to those who no longer need treatment (where hospitals "cure," hospices "care").

In a document called "To Live Each Day with Dignity," the bishops also note that "effective palliative care . . . allows patients to devote their attention to the unfinished business of their lives, to arrive at a sense of peace with God, with loved ones, and with themselves. No one should dismiss this time as useless or meaningless. Learning how to face this last stage of our earthly lives is one of the most important and meaningful things each of us will do, and caregivers who help people through this process are also doing enormously important work."

The Church's view is that hospices need to be extended and made more accessible, such that no one ever needs to die alone and in severe pain.

As the U.S. bishops' statement notes: "When we grow old or sick, and we are tempted to lose heart, we should be surrounded by people who ask, 'How can we help?' We deserve to grow old in a society that views our cares and needs with a compassion grounded in respect, offering genuine support in our final days. The choices we make together now will decide whether this is the kind of caring society we will leave to future generations. We can help build a world in which love is stronger than death."

This is not, it should be clear, about extending a life unnecessarily. It is not right zealously to provide burdensome treatment to extend a life when it is disproportionate to the relief it brings. Pain management — the specialism of hospice care — may even, sometimes, shorten a life. If the intention is not to kill but to alleviate suffering, even when death is a foreseen result of that intervention, that is not euthanasia. The purpose of palliative care is to provide an environment of love and support for a person on his or her final journey.

Still, no amount of palliative care will convince those who argue that dying is devoid of any intrinsic meaning (which, without God and an afterlife, it arguably is); who don't think death has any purpose beyond ending life; and for whom the indignity associated with the process should at all costs be avoided, whether or not it involves intense suffering. Advocates of a change in the law see this is a classic case of religious people trying to impose their own norms on other people through the coercive power of the state. And anyway, they argue, nothing they propose prevents anyone choosing, if the person wishes, to die a "natural" death.

But the Church's opposition to assisted dying is not an attempt to persuade people of no faith to adopt a religious view of death. Nor does it appeal to the right to die a natural death. The Church's opposition relies on a view of the common good of society, and how legalizing assisted suicide would undermine that good.

The law cannot, in reality, be neutral; either the law regards death as therapy, or it upholds the sacredness of all life. If participating in a suicide is legally and ethically acceptable, it can only be because there's a *right* to suicide; once we allow that such a right exists, the arguments for confining it to the dying seem arbitrary at best. In the same way, choosing to allow God or nature to take its course would over time come to be regarded as optional, eccentric, and even selfish.

As the U.S. bishops put it: "The assisted-suicide agenda promotes a narrow and distorted notion of freedom, by creating an *expectation* that certain people, unlike others, will be served by being helped to choose death. Many people with illnesses and disabilities who struggle against great odds for their genuine rights — the right to adequate health care and housing, opportunities for work and mobility, and so on — are deservedly suspicious when the freedom society most eagerly offers them is the 'freedom' to take their lives."

They add: "Those who choose to live may . . . be seen as selfish or irrational, as a needless burden on others, and even be encouraged to view themselves that way."

The Experience of Oregon

This is borne out by the experience of Oregon, where assisted suicide has been legal since 1998. Research has shown that at least one in six, and as many as one in four, of those seeking assisted suicide there are clinically depressed.

The regime in place, regarded as a model of best practices, has been monitored in annual reports by the Oregon Health Department (OHD). The figures for 2009 showed that there were 59 assisted suicides in that year, increasing from 49 in 2008. In total there have been 460 assisted suicides in the 12 years since the Oregon Death with Dignity Act (ODDA).

Although advocates are at pains to demonstrate that Oregon provides a death service for the terminally ill of all ages, not just the elderly, the Oregon reports tell a different story. The OHD's figures for 2009 show that the greatest resort to assisted suicide is in the 75-84 age group, and that the median age was 76. Nor are they always terminally ill. The top three reasons consistently given each year are "loss of autonomy due to illness," "loss of control of bodily functions," and "inability to participate in enjoyable activities." The numbers also show a rising trend in those citing reasons such as inadequate pain control and being a burden on friends and family.

These reasons demolish the assisted-suicide lobby's contention that assisted suicide is a means of escaping intolerable symptomatic suffering. It is being resorted to as a means of being in personal control over the dying process, by elderly people fearful of depending on others ("not wishing to be a burden on family, friends and caregivers" was a reason given by one-third of those who took their lives under Oregon's regime in 2008). There is real suffering behind the reasons cited, but pain does not rank high among them.

Applicants for assisted suicide must sign a form declaring that they make the application voluntarily and without reservation; and witnesses are needed to attest that the applicants are in sound mind and not under duress or any undue influence. But there is no procedure for ensuring that this still is the case when the drugs are actually taken — on average, 33 days after prescription, with a range (in 2004) of 15 to 593 days. In the meantime, patients can become depressed or subject to all kinds of pressures, whether external or inside their minds.

In his book *A Time to Live: The Case Against Euthanasia and Assisted Suicide*, George Pitcher summarizes the inadequacies of the Oregon model as follows:

1. The numbers seeking assisted suicide in Oregon are now four times as many as 12 years ago.
2. A large number of prescriptions for lethal drugs are being written not by the patient's regular doctor but by another doctor who is likely to be more sympathetic to assisted suicide. This suggests the emergence of a two-tier medical profession, with some doctors committed to end-of-life care and others to euthanasia.
3. The main incidence of assisted suicide in Oregon is among the elderly, one in four of whom, according to a *British Medical Journal* study in 2008, are depressed.

4. The increased number of people seeking assisted suicide to avoid being a burden on others shows the growth of internalized pressures and coercion.
5. Regulation of the ODDA is extremely loose and contains few safeguards to protect the vulnerable.

If Oregon is indeed a model of best practices, it shows precisely why an assisted-suicide law will encourage the elderly to take their lives.

The Autonomy Illusion

The moral case for assisted suicide rests, essentially, on the case for autonomy. It is axiomatic in the advocates' arguments that the individual must be the first and only judge of when the time is right for dying; and further, that this choice serves a greater good — the relief of a burden on others.

But this is a fallacious idea. Our human identity is wrapped up with other people, especially those whom we love and serve. In the radically individualist philosophy behind the case for assisted suicide, there is no objective value placed on life; the only value is the one I judge myself to have. And the premise is that a life loses value the closer it is to death. Once we lose the idea of life having an objective — Christians would say sacred — value, there is no reason why anyone should care for it.

Advocates of assisted suicide accept the need for legal and procedural safeguards to ensure that people are not being pressured or coerced into choosing suicide — in other words, to protect the "autonomy" of the decision. But in reality, decisions are never autonomous. The autonomy of a sick person, above all, is in flux: what people wish for will vary from day to day. And what a man or woman feels on the day of being given a terminal diagnosis may be quite different from what that person feels after experiencing quality palliative medicine. Understandably, psychiatrists are strongly opposed to being asked to carry out such assessments.

As Baroness Ilora Finlay, a British professor in palliative care and campaigner against assisted suicide, says: "In reality, the vast majority of people facing dying are ambivalent, oscillating between hopelessness and hope, worrying about being a financial or personal burden on those they love, or that their own care costs will erode their descendants' inheritance. In a word, they are vulnerable, and it is a primary purpose of any law to protect the weak and vulnerable, rather than to give rights to the strong and determined at their expense."

Put another way, keeping assisted suicide illegal is the best way of protecting the disabled, elderly, sick, depressed, or other vulnerable people from ending their lives for fear of being a financial, emotional, or care burden upon others.

Ironically, the idea of autonomy is sometimes abandoned completely in another argument in favor of assisted suicide — the way we put down our ailing pets. If the kindest thing to do with a suffering dog or cat is to put it out of its misery, how much kinder it would be, some argue, to do the same for a suffering human being. But this comparison simply doesn't bear scrutiny. Our animals do not have consciousness; precisely because their suffering cannot be meaningful to them, we take the responsibility to end their lives. It would be intolerable, in fact, to keep a suffering animal alive because we cannot bear to be parted from it. To suggest that the system we use for keeping animals should be transferred to human beings is to suggest that some human beings are like passive pets, to be disposed of at will because their lives are not judged to be worth preserving. That is precisely the attitude which euthanasia and assisted suicide bring about.

A Call for Better End-of-Life Care

The Catholic view is that behind the drive to legalize assisted dying is the positive intention of seeking freedom from *unnecessary suffering* — the suffering associated with the indignity of dying in a hospital, or the feeling of being a burden to others. These failures, which lie behind many of the calls to choose the time of dying, must be addressed — rather than acceded to through legalization, which would reinforce those failures.

Consider the Netherlands and Belgium, where euthanasia is legal and palliative-care provisions fall far below standards elsewhere. The architect of the 2001 Dutch euthanasia law, Els Borst, admitted in 2009 that the government of the time was wrong to have introduced euthanasia without improving palliative care. Now that euthanasia has become socially acceptable in the Netherlands — in 2008 Dutch doctors reported 2,331 cases of euthanasia and 400 cases of assisted suicide — the pressure to improve palliative care has considerably lessened. The Netherlands should be a warning to other countries. Persistent requests for euthanasia are very rare if people are properly cared for. But it's harder properly to care for people once euthanasia is allowed. Assisted suicide chills the environment for the dying, encouraging people to seek death as an alternative to the suffering they fear, or the burden they are worried they will be on others.

It also corrodes the general culture of life. To show how this happens, consider, again, Holland, where it is estimated that about one thousand people die a year as a result of physicians ending a patient's life *without* an explicit request at the time of death. These may be patients dying of cancer, or handicapped newborn babies, or, in 35 percent of cases, the reasons have simply not been recorded. Perhaps even more worryingly, only 54 percent of all euthanasias in Holland are reported to the authorities. Study after study shows that there are a large number of Dutch doctors who subscribe to the view that suffering is pointless, and who make unilateral decisions to terminate lives — just like the eugenicist and Chicago surgeon Harry Haiselden.

A change in the law might meet the demands of a small number of highly determined people with strong convictions about personal autonomy; but it would put a far larger number of infirm and vulnerable people at risk. We need to increase the quality of people's end-of-life care, not evade the challenge through euthanasia.

It is an irony that the demand for assisted suicide has appeared just at the time when it is unnecessary: since the 1970s, the rise of advanced palliative care has transformed the relief of extreme pain. Yet as the U.S. bishops point out, authorizing assisted suicide removes incentives for excellence in the palliative field, and results in the redirection of resources:

Government programs and private insurers may even limit support for care that could extend life, while emphasizing the "cost-effective" solution of a doctor-prescribed death. The reason for such trends is easy to understand. Why would medical professionals spend a lifetime developing the empathy and skills needed for the difficult but important task of providing optimum care, once society has authorized a "solution" for suffering patients that requires no skill at all? Once some people have become candidates for the inexpensive treatment of assisted suicide, public and private payers for health coverage also find it easy to direct life-affirming resources elsewhere.

Rather than defend the status quo, therefore, we need to be passionate reformers, but in the direction of improving the quality of the journey at the end of life, not suicide. This is especially necessary in a culture like ours, which puts an excessively high premium on values like productivity and cost savings.

Some of those reforms might need to be imaginative. Pope Benedict XVI, for example, has called assistance to the dying one of the great needs of our time, and suggested "dying leave," like maternity leave, so workers can spend time with close loved ones who are dying.

But, ultimately, this is an argument which has to return, inevitably, to the meaning of suffering and dying — and what it means to be human.

Doctors and nurses who work in end-of-life care know that there are many myths about dying. One is that doctors "speed up" the process by giving massive, fatal doses of morphine. In fact, morphine can extend life by controlling pain and breathlessness and making patients comfortable. Morphine does not kill. Just because there is a last dose of a drug does not mean that the drug causes death (you might as well blame the last cup of water). Equally, the removal of life support — apparatuses to assist breathing, or kidney or liver functions — does not cause death; when doctors decide to discontinue treatment, it is to allow the process of dying to take place, because death cannot be prevented. An end-of-life decision is different from a life-ending decision.

Doctors are trained to understand and manage the all-important transition from, on the one hand, treating a patient — supporting a body's functions long enough to allow a person to recover — and, on the other, acknowledging treatment that is futile and to not prevent the natural process of dying. A doctor's role, supported by the Hippocratic oath, is to support life as long as life has a chance. No wonder the medical profession overwhelmingly opposes assisted suicide and euthanasia.

Perhaps the most potent myth, and one that drives the call for assisted suicide, is that most deaths are painful and difficult, yet most are not. In fact, most deaths are comfortable, if spiritually and emotionally demanding on everyone involved. Yet deaths are not, on the whole, "dignified." The advocates of assisted suicide appeal constantly to the idea of "dignity in death" as something rational and controlled, like a decision to jump in the sea before the boat hits the rocks. Dying involves renunciation, pain, and many indignities. We are not in control. And it calls forth compassion — "suffering with" — in those who love and care for the person dying. Assisting a suicide is a corruption of compassion. A state that endorses it is creating an ominous new option which will rapidly undermine the sacred value of life itself.

∞

Existing Frame

"A dignified death, free of pain at a moment of our own choosing is now possible. Why should the Church interfere with the choice of people who want to relieve their own suffering or those of their loved ones? Palliative care has made great steps forward, but it is not always well applied, and people are still kept alive unnecessarily in great pain. There should be a law to allow mentally competent, terminally ill people who see no point in suffering to choose the time and manner of their departure."

Reframe

Assisted suicide is a mistaken attempt to avoid pain and suffering. The idea of autonomous, free, rational choice in favor of suicide is a myth. Rather than condemn people to unnecessary suffering, we need to enhance the quality of our care for the dying.

∞

Key Messages

Against changing the law:

- Assisted suicide gives the green light to hopelessness and despair. It sanctions suicide as a response to hardship. It leaves the vulnerable more vulnerable, especially the disabled, whose lives may be judged less valuable in law. The right to die will become a duty to die.

- It will destroy the trust between doctor and patient.
- The drive to change the law comes from a small group of determined individuals who view life as something that can and should be under our absolute control. They are sincere in their beliefs; but what matters here is what is good for society. The law must uphold life and protect the vulnerable.
- As the experience of the Netherlands shows, euthanasia undermines palliative care.

In favor of extending palliative care:

- A person who suffers is no less a person than one who doesn't. Some suffering in life will be unavoidable; it is part of the process of dying. But no one should nowadays endure unbearable pain.
- The English-speaking world leads the globe in hospices and palliative care. We need more, not fewer, of these. People suffering/in pain should be offered *real* choice — the choice not to suffer unnecessarily. Euthanasia does not solve that problem; it covers it up.

Chapter 5

CLERICAL SEX ABUSE

— Challenging Questions —

- *Why has it taken so long for the Church to take clerical sexual abuse seriously?*
- *Why were priests who had allegations of abuse against them routinely moved to other parishes where the abuse could continue?*
- *Why do bishops in some countries still blame the media rather than take the allegations seriously? And why aren't they reprimanded by Rome?*
- *What structures are in place to ensure that laicized priests don't simply disappear underground and continue to abuse children?*

Is the clerical sex abuse crisis, as some claim, the greatest threat to the Catholic Church since the Reformation? No. The mass executions of priests in the French and Mexican revolutions and 1930s Spain, or the wholesale suppression and persecution of the Church in Stalinist Russia, presented a more pressing challenge to Catholic existence.

But crisis it certainly has been — not least for Catholics themselves, who have been shocked and saddened by an almost constant stream of revelations. As the full body of the U.S. bishops said in June 2011:

> Since 2002, the Church in the United States has experienced a crisis without precedent in our times. The sexual abuse of children and young people by some deacons, priests, and bishops, and the ways in which these crimes and sins were addressed, have caused enormous pain, anger, and confusion. As bishops, we have acknowledged our mistakes and our roles in that suffering, and we apologize and take responsibility again for too often failing victims and the Catholic people in the past. From

the depths of our hearts, we bishops express great sorrow and profound regret for what the Catholic people have endured.

Media focus has been intense and incessant. The accusations — coverup of crimes, deafness to the voice of victims, sexual misconduct, abuse of trust — could hardly be worse. The conviction in newsrooms that the Church has been unaccountable, and needs to puts its house in order, has given the media a sense of moral entitlement in placing the Church under an unforgiving spotlight.

Without that spotlight, of course, the voice of the victims would not have been heard and vital reforms would never have happened — at least not as speedily, as the Archdiocese of Boston acknowledged in its January 2012 "Reflections" on ten years since the abuse crisis erupted there. "The media helped make our Church safer for children by raising up the issue of clergy sexual abuse and forcing us to deal with it," Cardinal Seán O'Malley wrote. "All of us who hold the protection of children as the highest priority are indebted to the media's advocacy on this issue."

But this does not excuse distortions, exaggerations, myths, ignorance, and lazy reporting, let alone the "gotcha" relish, which has characterized many of the stories. "What guided this press campaign was not only a sincere desire for truth," said Pope Benedict XVI in *Light of the World (LoW)*, "but there was also some pleasure in exposing the Church and, if possible, discrediting her." And yet, significantly he adds, "we must be grateful for every disclosure." The media has performed a necessary service.

From January 2002, the crisis exploded in the United States, beginning in the Archdiocese of Boston; for six months it was seldom off the front pages. In 2009, the focus was on Ireland following two devastating reports (Ryan and Murphy). In 2010, it shifted to Central Europe, and especially Germany. Mostly the scandals have concerned local churches; but the Vatican has been in the spotlight, especially for its failure to deal quickly or adequately — especially in the last years of Pope John Paul II — with two notorious cases, that of the former archbishop of Vienna, Cardinal Hans Gröer, and the Mexican founder of the Legionaries of Christ, Father Marcial Maciel Degollado.

The scandal has had four principal elements:

1. *A moral crisis*: revelations that priests used their status to manipulate and coerce young people into illegal and immoral sexual relations;

2. *an institutional crisis*, in which the desire to preserve the Church's good name led victims to being silenced or paid off while the perpetrators went unpunished;

3. *a crisis of local Church leadership*, as evidence emerges of bishops acting indulgently toward abusers and highhandedly toward victims — and above all, failing to reveal accusations to civil authorities;

4. *a crisis of universal Church leadership*, centered on accusations that Rome failed to force local bishops to take action against abusive priests, or even obstructed that action, while failing to act against very senior figures such as Gröer and Maciel.

What has been ignored or underreported by the news media are the countless ways in which the Church has sought to put its house in order through strict new guidelines and procedures, and tightening up on the internal Church mechanisms to punish perpetrators; all of which ensure that the crisis can never reoccur. Among the most important of these changes are:

1. Strict guidelines introduced by many — but not yet all — bishops' conferences across the world which mandate immediate reporting of any accusation to the police and social services, and the immediate suspension of the accused priest. An example of early action was taken by the Church in England and Wales, which in 2001 set up a commission under Lord Nolan which led to guidelines and procedures which have made it a model institution, held up by the government as an example for other institutions to follow. Soon after, the Dallas Norms introduced by the U.S. bishops led to far-reaching reforms based on the "zero tolerance" principle.

2. Vatican reforms beginning in 2001 which led to fast-track laicization of abusive priests, the lifting of a statute of limitations to enable the punishment of abuse many decades ago, and the obligation to notify Rome of any substantial allegations of abuse, to ensure action is taken. In 2010 canon law was further updated to ensure speedy justice for victims, and a letter was sent to all bishops' conferences urging the reporting of abuse cases to civil authorities.

3. Pope Benedict's letter to the Irish of March 19, 2010, possibly the most heartfelt apology ever offered by a pope, which led to a Vatican-

appointed delegation of cardinals to investigate dioceses and seminaries, and to put in place necessary reforms. The letter followed
two devastating reports in 2009 which highlighted chronic failures
in the Irish bishops' handling of abuse claims over many decades; the
reports led to the entire hierarchy being summoned to Rome, and
the resignations of a number of bishops.

There are many more examples. A Vatican web page, "Abuse of Minors: The Church's Response," is a useful compilation of actions and
documents from Rome.

The overall picture, therefore, is one of serious flaws and failings being painfully exposed, leading to vigorous and far-reaching reforms. In
Pope Benedict's words, it is "a call to recognize again our fundamental
values and to see the dangers that threaten not only priests but society as
a whole" (*LoW*, 41). This catharsis is evident in a new attitude and a new
resolve. Worldwide, much still remains to be done: having put in place
reforms to ensure that the crisis can never recur, the Church's focus is
now increasingly on the victims themselves, supporting them and helping them to heal, and placing the expertise and understanding gained at
the service of wider society.

03

Positive Intention

The positive intention behind the criticism of the Church couldn't be
clearer: the protection of children from sexual abuse. The perception is
that children were not and are not safe within the Church. The moral
value behind the indignation is a deeply Christian one: the abuse
of innocence, and the sacrifice of children on the altar of institutional
reputation, are in clear violation of everything the Gospel stands for.

03

Putting the Church's House in Order

The crisis is not over until every bishops' conference across the globe
ensures that allegations are never again swept under the carpet. And there
is still plenty of healing to do, together with compensation payouts. But

across the Western world — notably in the United States and the United Kingdom — reforms have been put in place by bishops which ensure that what happened in the 1960s-1980s cannot recur, reforms which make the Catholic Church in those countries a leader in safeguarding, to the point where the British government, for example, recommends the U.K. Catholic Church procedures to other institutions as a model to follow. In 2009 there were just six contemporary allegations of abuse against U.S. priests, in a Church of 65 million Catholics; in England and Wales, where Catholics number around 5 million, there were four allegations in 2007. The Church is an extremely safe institution for young people today.

The Vatican has asked for every bishops' conference in the world to draw up similar guidelines to ensure that the same will be said of the Church in other countries: better screening of candidates to the priesthood; the punishment (in both civil and canon law) of perpetrators; review of historical files to ensure that if action was not taken then it is taken now; and efforts to assist and support victims — all these are part of the Church's new approach. A new multi-institution e-learning center to help the Church throughout the world deal swiftly and effectively with clerical abuse of minors has been established in Munich, Germany.

This is a crisis about abuse which took place many decades ago which was, *back then*, mishandled. All the studies agree that clerical sexual abuse of minors increased from the mid-1960s through the late 1970s; it then declined in the 1980s, and remains very low. Ironically, it was not long after this sharp drop in abuse allegations against priests, in the 1980s, that victims started to step forward. They were generally in their thirties and forties, or older — a silent generation finding its voice in lawsuits and news reports. But the abuse itself had happened decades earlier. It was not until 2002-2003 that, following a relentless series of media stories, the Church began to search through its archives to find instances of abuse improperly dealt with or abusers who had gone unpunished. The resulting stories gave the impression that clerical abuse is current or recent; hence the widespread but wholly misleading perception that Church environments are not as safe as the facts indicate they are.

The reporting creates a further distortion by reading the past in the light of present-day sensibilities. Back when the abuse happened, a different social mentality prevailed: the issue was never discussed; the press did not investigate; victims were silenced or stayed silent out of shame. This was behavior typical of society as a whole, especially of institutions such as schools or orphanages. That does not make it right. But to describe this as a "coverup," which assumes a deliberate intention to conceal information from those who have a right to know about it, is to read the past through the lens of the present. It would have been extremely unusual, at the time when most of this abuse took place, for institutions to have reported it.

Nowadays, although there are exceptions — the diocese of Cloyne in Ireland was sharply criticized by both Church and state for failing to report allegations as late as 2009 — the Church in the West is now outstanding in reporting and making public any allegation, setting an example for other institutions and society as a whole.

The most detailed report into the abuse in Catholic institutions was commissioned in 2002 by the U.S. Catholic bishops from independent researchers, at a cost of $1.8 million. The highly regarded John Jay College of Criminal Justice in New York published the first part of its report, "The Nature and Scope of the Problem of Sexual Abuse of Minors by Catholic Priests and Deacons in the United States," in 2004; the second part, "The Causes and Context of Sexual Abuse of Minors by Catholic Priests in the United States, 1950-2010," came out in May 2011.

The report examined all plausible allegations of abuse of minors by clergy in the period between 1950 and 2002. The researchers used a very low standard of proof for the charges — "not withdrawn or known to be false" — rather than proof of guilt. Over that fifty-year period, the study found, 4,392 out of approximtely 100,000 clergy were accused — just over 4 percent of all priests. About 80 percent of the accusations were of abuse alleged to have occurred between the 1960s and the 1980s; more than half of those accused were accused of a single incident; and almost all the allegations concerned post-pubescent males — in other words, they were not allegations of pedophilia per se (although no less criminal and sinful). In total, there was an average of 200 accusations (not convictions) a year, although a closer examination of the statistics presents a more accurate picture. Just 149 individuals were responsible for a quarter of all abuse allegations. And 40 percent of the allegations date from a six-year period in late 1970s.

The second part of the report revealed that by the mid-1980s, bishops knew that abuse was a problem, but they had no idea of its extent.

"Though more than 80 percent of cases now known had already occurred by 1985, only 6 percent of those cases had been reported to the dioceses by that time," the report notes. The bishops simply did not know of the scale of the problem until much later — in fact, not until the 1990s. By this time the abuse itself had sharply decreased. This, incidentally, was exceptional. The report shows that while abuse increased in the Church at the same time as it increased in wider society, it decreased in the Church from the 1980s because of the actions taken by the Church at the time.

The report does not exculpate Church leaders, whose "response typically focused on the priest-abusers rather than on the victims." They remained ignorant, too, of the effect of sexual abuse because they did not often meet with victims before 2002; as knowledge of victim harm increased in society generally in the 1990s, so did the understanding by diocesan leaders. Among the report's other findings were these:

1. Although it is impossible to predict which men might abuse minors, certain factors — being abused as a child, stress, alcohol — contributed. Many priest abusers had difficulty in relating to adults.

2. Celibacy was not the cause of sexual abuse. The sexual abuse of minors by priests in the United States "increased steadily from the mid-1960s through the late 1970s, then declined in the 1980s and continued to remain low," the report notes; yet celibacy remained constant throughout this period.

3. Homosexuality was not the cause either. Although 81 percent of the victims of clergy abuse were male, there are no data to indicate that homosexual orientation is a cause or risk factor for abuse of minors.

4. Poor seminary formation played a significant role in the crisis. Most offenders were ordained before the 1970s, but did not generally abuse before then. Seminaries at the time had little or no exposure to a curriculum of what is now understood as "human formation": the training in self-understanding and the development of emotional and psychological competence for a life of celibate chastity. The coincidence of inadequate seminary formation and sexual laxity in wider society seems to be the major factor behind the prevalence of abuse.

The Catholic Church in the United States is these days an exceptionally safe place for young people. But there is still much healing to be done. As the Archdiocese of Boston said in "Ten Years Later," its reflections on the sexual abuse crisis of January 4, 2012:

> As an archdiocese, as a Church, we can never cease to make clear the depth of our sorrow and to beg forgiveness from those who were so grievously harmed. We also must acknowledge and express our gratitude for all that survivors and their loved ones have done, and continue to do, to help make the Church, and all of society, safer for children. We are humbled as many survivors have offered forgiveness to the Church and encouraged others to re-establish their relationship with the God who offers all of us the gifts of love and healing.

Explaining the Focus on the Church

Noting that no other institution had undertaken a public study of sexual abuse, the John Jay report urged other organizations to follow suit: "Only with such an understanding can effective prevention policies be articulated and implemented." In fact, little attention has been given to the wider social problem of abuse and the absence of transparency in other institutions. In the United States, for example, there is no obligation for a school to make public an allegation of sex abuse against a staff member. There has been a massive silence on this issue.

Yet the fact that the Church has received highly selective, disproportionate attention — some might say been "scapegoated" — doesn't make it innocent. There is no excuse for its failures to hear the voice of the victim decades ago. But equally, it is unfair to claim that Church-run institutions are hotbeds of abuse, or that the Catholic priesthood contains an exceptionally large number of abusers, or that the Church's "coverup" of allegations was uniquely pernicious. There is no credible evidence that Catholic clergy have abused young people at a rate different from the clergy of any other denomination, and much evidence that the rate is considerably lower than in secular professions which deal with children. But it is difficult to say exactly, because no other profession or church has conducted a systematic survey in the way that the Catholic Church has.

One of the few there have been — into schools — took place over seven months by the Associated Press in 2007. AP's research revealed that sex abuse of children in U.S. schools was widespread, and mostly unreported (or "covered up"): It found "2,570 educators whose teaching credentials were revoked, denied, surrendered, or sanctioned from 2001 through 2005 following allegations of sexual misconduct." Professor Charol Shakeshaft of Virginia Commonwealth University studied 290,000 cases of alleged abuse between 1991 and 2000; out of a sample of 225 teachers who admitted sexually abusing a pupil, not a single one had been reported to the authorities.

If the Church has not been uniquely, or even especially, defective in dealing with abuse, why has it been singled out, scrutinized as no other institution has been? Much of the reporting reflects a prejudice in society about celibacy as "unnatural," leading to the idea that celibate priests need a sexual "escape valve." Yet some 70 percent of abuse of minors takes place within families, by married men. And there is no evidence that there is less abuse by married pastors in the Protestant or Anglican traditions. The 4 percent figure identified by the John Jay study is consistent with male clergy from other traditions and significantly lower than the general male adult population (which is estimated at best to be around 8 percent).

The main explanation for the intense focus on the Church lies in the way the cases first came to light. Because no other organization has as many parishes, schools, and orphanages, and because dioceses keep meticulous records that yield a reliable portrait of its personnel and abuse over the decades, the Church has been an obvious target for civil litigation. An individual accuses a priest of abuse; lawyers then use that case as a means of forcing a diocese to disclose its files on other abuse allegations, which then become the basis for a network of interlocking cases — and news stories. Most religious institutions are more decentralized, smaller, and therefore harder to analyze or prosecute; few have assets on the scale of a Catholic diocese. That is one reason why it has been considered justifiable, economically and practically, for lawyers on behalf of claimants to bring civil claims against the Catholic Church rather than against other institutions.

In the 1990s a growing number of lawsuits were settled by dioceses through settlements accompanied by confidentiality agreements. Because the priest perpetrators were frequently left unpunished, when these settlements later came to light the media could easily portray them as proof that the Church was "buying the victims' silence." As lawyers began mounting more and more actions, a picture began to emerge of bishops failing to report abuse allegations and instead moving priests between parishes following those allegations; encountering an often dismissive and highhanded response, the media scented blood.

Accounting for Failure

In January 2002, the crisis exploded in the United States after the *Boston Globe* persuaded judges to force the Archdiocese of Boston to make public its confidential files. What emerged was a sorry picture of inaction, denial, and confidential settlements that meant that the story was rarely off the front pages until June that year, when the U.S. bishops in Dallas introduced far-reaching reforms, including the John Jay study mentioned above. In order to put a stop to the hugely damaging drip-drip of lawsuits, the bishops agreed to review their diocesan files to ensure that any allegation would now be acted upon. In December 2002, Boston's Cardinal Bernard Law resigned.

How had these failures come about? There is no doubt that in a confined period (around the 1960s-1970s) abuse took place within the priesthood — anywhere between 1,000 and 3,000 priests in the United States sexually engaged with minors. Although this figure is consistent with rates of abuse by male clergy of other denominations, and considerably less than the male adult population in general, it is still a shocking number.

One reason is that the priesthood was far easier to enter 30 years ago. As Thomas Plante, professor of psychology at Santa Clara University, writes in his 2010 study, "A Perspective on Clergy Sexual Abuse":

> Thirty years ago, most priests entered seminary during high school, did not participate in a comprehensive psychological evaluation prior to admission, and had no training in sexuality, maintaining professional boundaries, and impulse control.

Advice regarding dealing with sexual impulses included cold showers and prayer. Today, most applicants to the priesthood are much older (generally in their late 20s and 30s). They have often had satisfying and appropriate intimate relationships before entering the seminary. They have completed a psychological evaluation that specifically examines risk factors for sexual problems. They now get good training in sexuality and issues related to managing sexual impulses. It is not surprising that the majority of the sex-offending priests that we hear about in the press are older. In fact, our research indicates that the average age of these men is 53.

Then there was the failure by bishops to act on allegations and punish the perpetrators. As John Jay shows, bishops in the early 1980s had no idea of the scale of the problem. And the prevailing psychiatric wisdom of the time was that pedophilia was an illness that could be managed or controlled with medication and therapy.

Yet the reluctance of bishops to punish sexually abusive priests seems remarkable today.

A common myth is that bishops resorted to canon rather than civil law in dealing with abusive priests, and that canon law had no real sanctions. In fact, canon law demands that a bishop investigate an allegation of sexual abuse and, if true, expel the abuser from the priesthood — something that should occur parallel to, not instead of, prosecution by police. Yet neither happened. The use of the penalties in the Church's own law had fallen into disuse. After the mid-1960s in Ireland, notes Pope Benedict in *Light of the World*, ecclesiastical penal law "was simply not applied anymore. The prevailing mentality was that the Church must not be a Church of laws, but rather, a Church of love; she must not punish. Thus the awareness that punishment can be an act of love ceased to exist. This led to an odd darkening of the mind, even in very good people."

The Murphy Commission report into the Archdiocese of Dublin's mishandling of abuse allegations from the 1960s to the 1980s found that none of its four archbishops ever reported the abuse that was brought to their attention, and that no canonical trials ever took place. The report documents a "collapse of respect for canon law. . . . Offenders were neither prosecuted nor made accountable within the Church." The normal response was for a bishop to send an abusive priest for therapy, in line with the thinking of the time — that pedophilia was a kind of psychological illness that could be cured. Later, it would be seen as a "fixation" or "orientation" that resisted therapy. The problem, however, was not with the use of therapy per se, but the way it was used as an alternative to punishing acts criminal in both civil and canon law.

In his *Pastoral Letter to the Catholics of Ireland* of March 19, 2010, Pope Benedict XVI addressed this specific failure of the bishops.

> It cannot be denied that some of you and your predecessors failed, at times grievously, to apply the long-established norms of canon law to the crime of child abuse. Serious mistakes were made in responding to the allegations. I recognize how difficult it was to grasp the extent and complexity of the problem, to obtain reliable information and to make the right decisions in the light of conflicting expert advice. Nevertheless, it must be admitted that grave errors of judgment were made and failures of leadership occurred. All this has seriously undermined your credibility and effectiveness.

But there were also obstacles in Rome to the most extreme punishment in canon law — the laicization of priests. One of the reasons that bishops around the world typically did not try to laicize abusive priests during the 1980s and 1990s was because the legal procedures for doing so were perceived as lengthy, cumbersome, and uncertain. Although it falls to the local bishop to act against an abusive priest — by suspending him, reporting him to the authorities, and so on — the procedure for laicizing him is reserved to Rome. Petitions for dispensation from the obligations of priesthood were sent to the Congregation for the Doctrine of the Faith (CDF), headed by Cardinal Ratzinger from 1980 until 2005.

Cardinal Ratzinger succeeded in persuading Pope John Paul II to give the CDF greater powers for dealing with abuse cases. In a 2001 *motu propio* (a change to the law on the pope's personal initiative) of Pope John Paul (called *Sacramentorum sanctitatis tutela*), two vital reforms were introduced: bishops were asked to forward directly to the CDF all credible cases of abusive priests, to ensure action was taken; second, the laicization process was fast-tracked so that abusive priests could be laicized by means of decree rather than a Church court trial. The reforms were further tightened in 2003 and 2010.

Prior to those reforms, the laicization of abusive priests took too long. Yet it is not true that these delays somehow enabled the priests in each case to continue abusing. Suspension and laicization are two separate actions. The first can be done by a bishop, with immediate effect; the second is a lengthy process that involves Rome. Suspension — meaning a priest is no longer able to function as a priest: say Mass, hear confessions, act as chaplain, etc. — is the key action that a bishop has to take against an abusive priest to prevent him from having contact with minors. It was wrong that abusers remained in the priesthood, and this was put right with the 2001 reforms. But even before then there is no evidence that delays in laicization enabled or encouraged priests to continue abusing.

Canon Law, Civil Law

The changes introduced by Cardinal Ratzinger in 2001 mean that nowadays clergy convicted (in civil courts) of sex abuse of minors — or where the evidence of that abuse is overwhelming — are swiftly expelled from the priesthood by means of an "*ex officio*" dismissal signed by the pope, without any need for a lengthy Church trial. Even in cases where the police have dropped charges (for lack of evidence, say) the Church still proceeds with its own investigation and trials. After reviewing the evidence, the CDF might authorize the local bishop to conduct either a full penal trial (before a local Church tribunal) or an "administrative penal process" which does not involve a trial. If the priest is judged guilty, canonical penalties may be imposed, including laicization.

These canonical processes occur alongside — in fact, almost always after — the investigation, trial, and conviction of the abusive priest by the police of that country. Civil and canon penalties are not alternatives. They exist in two parallel spheres; each has jurisdiction the other lacks. For example, civil law is capable of punishing by imprisoning while Church law is not; but Church law can laicize a priest, which is not something civil law can do. A possible analogy — one easily understood in the professional world — is that of associations or clubs with their own internal regulations. A lawyer who commits fraud will be investigated by police and, if guilty, sentenced to a term in prison. But he will also be subject to punishment by the bar association, which will withdraw his membership.

These are separate jurisdictions: the bar association cannot imprison the offender; the civil courts cannot strike him off the bar association list of *bona fide* lawyers. Each jurisdiction has its own sanctions. Action or inaction in one jurisdiction does not prevent action or inaction in the other. The bar association might decide to expel a member for conduct which brings the legal profession into disrepute, even when this conduct has not involved breaking any law or when the police have decided not to pursue the matter. In the same way, the Church will often choose to pursue an allegation when civil authorities have not. And even when the police have dropped charges against a priest, the accused priest must still go through a rigorous process of "risk assessment" by Church-appointed experts before he is allowed back into his parish.

Why does the Vatican not instruct bishops across the world to report any allegation they receive to the civil authorities? First, there is no need: the assumption of canon law is always that civil law be obeyed. As the Vatican's guidelines for understanding CDF procedures makes clear: "Civil law concerning reporting of crimes to the appropriate authorities should always be followed." But faced with evidence that bishops in different parts of the world have been less than keen to divulge cases to the police and social services, why does the Vatican not mandate that they do so? Rome does, indeed, "encourage" reporting every accusation to civil authorities. But *mandating* such reporting would be impossible, given the wide variety of legal circumstances in which the Church operates — in totalitarian states, for example, or in countries where abuse of minors is not a crime.

There are many myths about the 2001 document issued by Cardinal Ratzinger. It has often been claimed that this "ordered a coverup" by insisting that parties to an abuse allegation observe secrecy under pain of excommunication. *De Delictis Gravioribus* (2001) updated an earlier (1962) canonical document, *Crimen Sollicitationis*, which lawyers in the United States bringing claims on behalf of abuse victims have tried to use as evidence of a coverup of abuse ordered by the Vatican.

Yet the document was concerned with a specifically canonical crime — namely, the use of the confessional to solicit sexual favors. It imposes strict confidentiality during the trial and investigation precisely to allow the victims to give evidence freely and to protect the accused until found guilty — in other words, to ensure action is taken. These regulations are entirely within the jurisdiction of canon law. There is nothing in that document preventing victims reporting the case to their local police, and the assumption is that they would.

Ignorance of canon law, or the misreading of it to try to claim that the Church had a systematic policy of obstructing civil law, is at the origin of many of the false accusations against the Church in general, and Pope Benedict in particular, over clerical sex abuse. The Church needs to do a much better job of explaining what canon law is, and the media need to do a better job of researching before uncritically reproducing wild allegations.

Rome Takes Charge

Until the year 2000, the clerical sex abuse crisis was confined to the local Church — a matter that needed to be tackled by bishops, rather than by the Vatican. But a few high-profile, damaging cases put the spotlight on Rome. Although Pope John Paul II met American cardinals in 2002 to discuss the U.S. clerical sex abuse crisis, before his death in 2005 there was a tendency for cardinals in Rome to blame the media, or to see abuse as an "Anglo-Saxon" problem. A clear exception was Cardinal Ratzinger, who unsuccessfully sought to persuade Pope John Paul II to take action in two cases — those of Gröer and Maciel.

Cardinal Hans Hermann Gröer, archbishop of Vienna from 1986 to 1995, was forced to step down after various former students and monks came forward to accuse him of molesting them. Austria's statute of limitations meant he could not be prosecuted. In 1998, Cardinal Ratzinger sought to persuade Pope John Paul to investigate, but this was blocked by the then-secretary of state, Cardinal Angelo Sodano. As a result, although he was suspended as an abbot, Cardinal Gröer, who died in 2003, was never laicized.

An even more notorious case was that of Father Marcial Maciel Degollado, the Mexican founder of an order of more than 600 priests, the Legionaries of Christ, and its lay arm, Regnum Christi. From 1956 he led a double life, constantly engaged in financial and sexual misconduct and drug abuse, maintaining relationships with at least two women and fathering six children, two of whom he abused. Former members had made accusations of sexually abusive acts by Maciel since the 1980s. Finally, in 2001, the Congregation for the Doctrine of the Faith began to investigate.

In 2005, after Pope Benedict's election, his successor at the CDF, Cardinal William Levada, suspended Maciel, then 84, from ministry; he was ordered to live a life of prayer and penitence. A canonical trial was ruled out because of his advanced age. He died in 2008. In 2009, the Vatican appointed a panel of five bishops to investigate the order. In March 2010, the Legionaries admitted that their founder had been guilty of abuse and illicit relationships, and apologized. Maciel was formally denounced by the Vatican in 2010 for creating a "system of power" built on silence and obedience that enabled him to lead an "immoral" double life "devoid of scruples and authentic religious sentiment," which allowed him to abuse boys unchecked over many decades. The Vatican also acknowledged the "hardships" faced by Maciel's accusers over many years when they were ostracized or ridiculed, and commended their "courage and perseverance to demand the truth."

Since his election as pope in 2005, Benedict has moved decisively on the issue — introducing reforms, clearing Vatican logjams, issuing statements, and on his foreign trips, meeting abuse victims. The massive increase in activity from the Vatican on this issue can be seen on the Vatican web page dedicated to documenting the Church's response to abuse. Among the pontifical documents are more than a dozen by Pope Benedict, compared with two by Pope John Paul II.

Summarizing the pope's record on this issue, Gregory Erlandson and Matthew Bunson write in *Pope Benedict XVI and the Sexual Abuse Crisis*:

> From leading the CDF's efforts before and after 2001 in reviewing the case files of suspect priests to his own efforts to address the issue forthrightly as pope, Benedict has grown into a leadership role on this issue just when the Church most needed him. He has met with victims. He has rebuked the abuser priests. He has challenged the bishops. He has overseen a series of procedural reforms that have allowed the Church to respond more quickly when it is necessary to restrict, suspend or even laicize a priest.

Safe Environment in the United States

During his 2008 visit to the United States, Pope Benedict XVI spoke passionately, both on the plane as he traveled across the Atlantic, and in almost every public address, about the immense suffering and "shame" the Church felt over the sexual abuse of minors by clerics and a bishops' response that was "sometimes very badly handled."

Benedict XVI met for the first time with victims of abuse — poignantly from Boston, where the scandal first exploded — and during a meeting with the country's bishops, praised them for "attach[ing] priority to showing compassion and care to the victims." He noted, "Now that the scale and gravity of the problem is more clearly understood, you have been able to adopt more focused remedial and disciplinary measures and to promote a safe environment that gives greater protection to young people."

What are some of those measures?

1. According to numbers from the U.S. bishops' annual audit from 2009, Safe Environment training is taking place in 193 dioceses/eparchies of the country. More than 2.1 million clergy, employees, and volunteers in parishes and schools have been trained to recognize the behavior of offenders and instructed what to do about it. More than 5.2 million children have been trained to recognize abuse and protect themselves. The Church has run background checks on more than 1,887,000 volunteers and employees, 166,000 educators, 52,000 clerics, and 6,000 candidates for ordination. Men who feel a calling to the priesthood also now undergo extensive psychological testing before being admitted to seminary programs.

2. All dioceses have Codes of Conduct spelling out what is acceptable and unacceptable behavior, and encouraging the reporting of suspicious behavior.

3. All dioceses have Victim Assistance Coordinators, and their names and contact information are listed on the website of the U.S. bishops' conference. In 2009, $6.5 million was spent on therapy for the victims of clergy sexual abuse.

4. All dioceses have Safe Environment Coordinators to ensure ongoing compliance to the Charter for the Protection of Children and

Young People that the bishops adopted in 2005 and re-approved as a full body in June 2011. The names and contact information of the coordinators are listed on the bishops' conference website.

5.   Each diocese also has a Review Board — to which all allegations of abuse are reported — made up of people drawn from relevant professions such as the police, the probation services, social services, health, and the law. Religious orders have similar structures.

6.   Nationally, the Church has a Secretariat of Child and Youth Protection, whose task is to assist dioceses in setting up safe environment programs, develop and maintain audit mechanisms to ensure compliance, and prepare a public annual report describing the compliance of each diocese to the Charter's provisions.

7.   Since 2002, there has been a "zero tolerance" policy on abusers. When even a single act of sexual abuse by a priest or deacon is admitted or is established, the offending priest or deacon is removed permanently from ecclesiastical ministry, and, if the case warrants, dismissed from the clerical state.

8.   Around the country, bishops have met with abuse victims and dioceses have held "healing Masses."

ଔ

EXISTING FRAME

"The Catholic Church, both locally and in Rome, ignored and covered up the clerical sex abuse of children by priests for decades and continues to do so. It sought to silence the victims and refused to take action. Pope Benedict is particularly culpable in the coverup. Celibate priests are more likely to abuse children than others. The Church is an organization that continues to be hostile to media revelations and is still a dangerous place for children."

REFRAME

The appalling crime of clerical sex abuse of minors is a profound betrayal of priests' calling and the Gospel. For many years, the Church, like other institutions, failed to grasp the extent of sexual abuse and its compulsive nature; decades ago, it mishandled accusations and failed to punish perpetrators. But in the past 10 years, it has gone further than any other institution in putting in place vital reforms to ensure it can never happen again. Those reforms have made the Church transparent, accountable, and one of the safest places for young people. From 2001, when John Paul II gave him responsibility for dealing with sex abuse cases, Cardinal Ratzinger/Pope Benedict has led the reforms from the Vatican to ensure that across the world the Church will never again cover up or fail to hear the voice of the victims. The apologies from Church leaders — the pope, cardinals, bishops — have been forthright and thorough, and, most importantly, they have taken action. In the United States the system of safeguarding is exceptional, and recommended as a model for other institutions to follow. Increasingly, that can also be said of the Church in other countries, too.

ଓଷ

Key Messages

- *Moral awakening.* Society and its institutions have awakened to the prevalence of sex abuse of minors. Like other institutions thirty to forty years ago, Catholic schools and parishes did not act on allegations and the victims were not heard. There has been a sea change in the Church's attitudes and policies.
- *Media has helped the Church to change.* The media's job is to probe and to hold to account, and they have shone a light on some dark corners in the Church, which has spurred the Church to change its attitudes and procedures. Many of the reports have been hysterical and misleading. But we don't resent or reject the media holding us to account; we want to help them get their facts right.
- *Priesthood not a haven for abusers.* The Catholic priesthood is not, nor has it ever been, exceptional in the number of abusers in its ranks. There is no causal link between priestly celibacy and clerical sex abuse. The Church is now much more careful about candidates it accepts to the priesthood.
- *U.S. Church safe environment for young people.* The system of safeguarding is exceptional, and recommended as a model for other institutions to follow. Independent oversight is built in at every stage, and all allegations, however old, are automatically referred to police and social services.

- *No conflict between canon and civil law*. One isn't above or below the other. Put simply, all Catholics must obey the law — that's what canon law itself calls for. Both civil law and canon law regard the sexual abuse of minors as an extremely serious crime. The big difference between now and thirty years ago is that the Church acts on both laws, reporting allegations to police *and* to the Vatican.
- *Pope Benedict's lead in reforming the Vatican's approach*. Both as cardinal and as pope he has spearheaded vigorous reforms, acting decisively to combat what has been sometimes a culture of denial. He has made vital changes to Church law to ensure that perpetrators are swiftly punished.

Chapter 6

DEFENDING THE UNBORN

— Challenging Questions —

- *Would the Catholic Church want abortion to be illegal? Isn't it a woman's right to choose?*
- *Why does the Church put its dogma before the medical benefits of embryonic research?*

The Catholic Church's defense of unborn lives is probably its best-known public position. Because of the searing and heated debates over abortion in Western countries in the past decades, the Church has often found itself in the frame of an often lonely promoter of the rights of human life, which contemporary society fails to recognize.

But the Church cares about unborn human life in many other areas too: wherever it is experimented on, cloned, created, and killed — that is, treated as a mere "bunch of cells" instead of a God-created early human life, deserving of respect. In recent years, the Church and pro-life groups have opposed laws allowing scientists to perform experiments on human embryos created by in-vitro fertilization (IVF), together with embryo selection on the basis of gender and genes ("designer babies").

Despite occasional rare victories, the pro-life movement has been consistently defeated in its attempts to awaken society to the value and dignity of unborn lives. Catholics often feel powerless to alter what can seem like an inexorable slide. And it can often seem as if the prophetic voice pointing to the humanity of the silent unborn victim — whether the 12- or 20-week-old baby destroyed by suction methods, or the cluster of human cells in the petri dish, a complete human being in its early stage — is simply ignored by a society as too disturbing. Placing an absolute value on autonomy (a woman's right to terminate a pregnancy if she chooses; the promise of cures for Parkinson's), society is growing more, not less, deaf to cries on behalf of the voiceless victims.

But there is a bigger view. The direction of Western cultural history, indelibly marked by Christianity, is toward the eventual revelation of the humanity of the victim. Just as the voices of the slave, the ostracized foreigner, the battered housewife, the disabled, and the child-abuse victim have all, eventually, been heard, so will, eventually, the voice of the literally voiceless — the unborn child.

There are many signs that Western society is beginning to awaken from its deafness: surveys show increasing discomfort with the prevalence and frequency of abortion, and the price that has been paid since legalization in 1973. Empathy with the embryo — rather than the 10-week-old child in the womb — is not yet apparent to the same degree. But it is a matter of time.

On this issue, therefore, we need not accept the frame that we are opposing women's rights or scientific advance. Nor should anyone feel obliged to assert the "rights" of the embryo against the "rights" of adult human beings, as if this were a question of competing claims. Rather, we should imagine ourselves in the position of anti-slave-trade campaigners in the first years of the nineteenth century, knowing that society will eventually awaken to the humanity of beings which at the moment many refuse to see.

℅

POSITIVE INTENTION

Abby Johnson, the abortion clinic director turned pro-life campaigner, says in her book UnPlanned *that she "had never been interested in promoting abortion. I'd come to Planned Parenthood eight years before, believing that its purpose was primarily to prevent unwanted pregnancies, thereby reducing the number of abortions. That had certainly been my goal. And I believed that Planned Parenthood saved lives—the lives of women who, without the services provided by this organization, might resort to some back-alley butcher."*

Most advocates of legal abortion do not see it primarily as an ideological issue of women's rights or of personal autonomy, but as the best of alternatives. Abortion, they believe, frees a woman from an unplanned pregnancy; and keeping it legal at least prevents back-street abortions.

The positive value in favor of legal abortion is therefore compassion —
the same emotion which leads people to support embryonic stem-cell
research on the grounds that it may lead to cures.

ભ

Life from the Start

The Church has always opposed abortion, in spite of debate in the early
and medieval Church about when human beings acquired souls ("en-
soulment"). Even in the Middle Ages, when most Western Christians
did not see the early embryo as fully human, it was believed the human
embryo should never be attacked deliberately, however extreme the
circumstances.

This condemnation of abortion was anchored in the Church's reflection on Scripture. In the Old Testament, Exodus and the Psalms,
among other books, reveal a God who knows his creatures even before
they are born, and who forms, names, and loves the child in the womb.
At the heart of the Church's advocacy is this knowledge of God as the
author of our being. As the Congregation for the Doctrine of the Faith
summarized in the 1987 document *Donum Vitae*: "Human life is sacred
because from its beginning it involves 'the creative action of God' and
it remains forever in a special relationship with the Creator, who is its
sole end. God alone is the Lord of life from its beginning until its end:
No one can, in any circumstance, claim for himself the right to destroy
directly an innocent human being." That is why, at the Second Vatican
Council, *Gaudium et Spes* described abortion and infanticide as "abomi-
nable crimes."

But you don't need to believe in God to think that life should be
preserved. It is an observable, scientific fact that life begins in the womb.
The question is what value should be placed on unborn life relative to
other lives. The notion that every human life is intrinsically precious, and
not of greater or lesser value according to its stage of development (or
other characteristics), is a basic tenet of human-rights doctrine. What the
Catholic Church teaches, that human life is not of lesser value because
younger and less developed, is the foundational principle of a civilized

society. As the pro-life office of the U.S. bishops' conference puts it:

> Given the *scientific* fact that a human life begins at conception, the only moral norm needed to understand the Church's opposition to abortion is the principle that *each and every human life has inherent dignity, and thus must be treated with the respect due to a human person.* This is the foundation for the Church's social doctrine, including its teachings on war, the use of capital punishment, euthanasia, health care, poverty, and immigration. Conversely, to claim that some live human beings do *not* deserve respect or should *not* be treated as "persons" (based on changeable factors such as age, condition, location, or lack of mental or physical abilities) is to deny the very idea of *inherent* human rights. Such a claim undermines respect for the lives of many vulnerable people before and after birth.

Abortion as Eugenics

The abortion question is really two questions: the wrongness/licitness of abortion itself; and what the law and the state should determine.

Few argue that abortion is a moral *good*. The case in favor of moral abortion is first a philosophical one — that women have the right to determine for themselves whether to give birth to a child or interrupt their pregnancy — and second a pragmatic one: given that unplanned pregnancies are inevitable, and that women will always seek abortions, those who do so should not be criminalized or forced into the hands of "back-alley butchers."

This was the practical argument in favor of *Roe v. Wade*, although the effect has been to go far beyond decriminalizing the desperate acts of women seeking back-street terminations, to a point where abortion is now a socially acceptable (even if seldom discussed) backup to failed contraception. According to a study published by the Guttmacher Institute (formerly a division of Planned Parenthood), 54 percent of the U.S. women who had an abortion in 2000-2001 had been using a contraceptive method during the month they became pregnant. And of the 638,790 women reported to have had abortions in 2008, according to the Centers for Disease Control and Prevention, 44 percent had undergone one or more previous abortions.

The question is no longer, therefore, "Should we condemn women to have back-street abortions?" but rather, "Should the state continue to sanction the massive disposal of innocent human life?"

Similarly, the argument of autonomy — women should have the freedom to determine the outcome of their pregnancies — cannot be considered in isolation from the uses to which that freedom is being put, and the effect on society of those decisions.

The movement in favor of abortion was initially led by eugenicists: it was one of the methods they wanted to use to reduce the "rising tide of color" in America's streets. *Roe v. Wade* achieved their ambition. "Birth control and abortion are turning out to be great eugenic advances of our time," commented Frederick Osborn, founder of the Office of Population Research at Princeton and one of the leaders of the American Eugenics Society. "If they had been advanced for eugenic reasons, it would have retarded or stopped their acceptance."

The decision to terminate a pregnancy is frequently made after learning that a baby is disabled, often in the doctor's office where a woman discovers a disability through a prenatal scan. Medical staff will often suggest it at this point, and the abortion is carried out as a matter of routine; few will ever know. In this way, the termination of those society deems unfit or burdensome is being carried out daily, on a very large scale, thus fulfilling, by a series of individual choices, the ambitions of the early twentieth-century eugenicists.

In a speech to a pro-life group in 2011, Bishop James D. Conley, apostolic administrator of the Denver archdiocese, spoke of the legalization of abortion, and the resulting deaths of 50 million unborn children, as an example of "the violence of the strong against the weak." He said, "The strong decide what is right or wrong — even who lives and who dies."

The "weak" here include not just the disabled, but also the poor and minorities. Abortion, notes Dennis Sewell in his book *The Political Gene*, "has had a greater impact in reducing births among the economically disadvantaged than the middle class, and is proportionately more frequently carried out on women from racial minorities in the United States."

The Guttmacher Institute acknowledges that the abortion rate for black women is nearly five times that for white women, but attributes the discrepancy, in somewhat circular fashion, to black women having "higher unintended pregnancy rates." That may also help explain research suggesting that abortion clinics and referral agencies are disproportionately located in neighborhoods with high minority populations — it makes good business sense, even without any explicit eugenic intent.

This was illustrated in 2011 figures released by the New York City Department of Health — the first detailed statistics on abortions performed in the city. The numbers showed that 41 percent of all New York pregnancies (except those that ended in miscarriages) ended in abortion — far higher than the national average. More disturbing, but receiving far less media attention, was what the statistics revealed about the demography of New York abortions: the ZIP codes with the highest abortion rates overwhelmingly were also minority neighborhoods. Nearly 60 percent of non-Hispanic black pregnancies ended in abortion. New York's Cardinal Timothy M. Dolan called the data "downright chilling," and took part in an ecumenical media campaign to remind New Yorkers of the churches' crisis pregnancy resources. "New York does not deserve the gravestone 'Abortion capital of the world,'" he said. "Our boast is the Statue of Liberty, not the Grim Reaper."

Alveda Scott King, a black pro-life activist who is the niece of the civil-rights leader Martin Luther King Jr., joined other black leaders in New York a week later to support the role of crisis pregnancy centers in the Big Apple. She described attempts by the City Council to ban them as "an ongoing reflection of Margaret Sanger's racist eugenics, the genocidal greedy desire to eliminate what she called 'undesirables.'"

King also offered public support for a bill introduced in the House of Representatives at the end of 2011 called the Prenatal Nondiscrimination Act, which would have banned abortions performed because of the race or sex of the baby. "There's still a place in America where people can be killed because of their race, and the perpetrators go free. It's the abortion clinic," she said. "The minority baby whose mother listens to an abortionist who masks his racism in false compassion can be denied his life and liberty simply because of his skin color. This outrageous racism should be illegal."

A Growing Empathy

There has also been a gradual but growing reaction against the prevalence and ease of access to abortion. A 2009 Gallup poll, carried out every year since 1995, found for the first time that a majority of Americans self-identified as "pro-life" rather than "pro-choice." It also found that those who think all abortion should be illegal (23 percent) for the first time topped the number of those who think there should be no legal restrictions at all (22 percent). While those numbers were not repeated in the subsequent two years of polling, they prompted considerable soul-searching by abortion-rights advocates.

At the same time, the ground of the abortion debate has shifted markedly in the last decade or so, away from a zero-sum clash between the "right to choose" and the "right to life." Increasingly, studies reveal the harm done by abortion to women, as well as men, who suffer searing grief and regret for many years afterward.

But what may be most causing this rethink is science, which is revealing the wondrous humanity of the unborn child.

The so-called walking in the womb 3-D ultrasound films by British professor Stuart Campbell, made public in 2004, have markedly shifted public opinion. Campbell, an atheist, pro-choice doctor who used to perform abortions, is very far from being a pro-life campaigner; yet as a result of what he has seen through ultrasound technology he has become an outspoken advocate of reducing the legal upper limit in the United Kingdom. At the fetal growth stage in which nearly 10 percent of abortions are carried out (between ten and twelve weeks; another 10 percent are performed even later), the unborn child can clearly be seen "smiling," "walking," and feeling pain: a fully formed human being. Developments in ultrasound technology have made it impossible, now, to conceal what an abortion actually involves.

Frances Kissling, the former president of Catholics for Choice, and Kate Michelman, the former president of NARAL Pro-Choice America, acknowledged in a 2010 *Washington Post* op-ed that an increasing number of Americans described themselves as "pro-life," and attributed this shift to those ultrasound pictures. "Neither [the pro-life nor pro-choice] movement can take full credit or blame for the change," they wrote. "Science played a big role, making the fetus more visible. Today, the first picture in most baby books is the twelve-week 3-D ultrasound, and Grandma and Grandpa have that photo posted on the fridge."

The revelation of that humanity has made the traditional yardsticks for determining the legality of abortion seem even more arbitrary. Because of the language of *Roe v. Wade*, the legal upper limit for abortion has been traditionally determined by the idea of "viability" — that is, when life can be sustained outside the womb, independent of the mother — and some states specifically name, on this basis, the number of weeks (usually twenty-four) after which abortions are illegal. Congress passed the Partial-Birth Abortion Ban Act in 2003, outlawing a particularly gruesome procedure that usually takes place at fifteen to twenty-six weeks (that is, pre- and post-viability) and involves delivering the fetus halfway, to its navel, before "disarticulating" the neck with a pair of scissors. The ban was upheld by the Supreme Court in 2007.

Six states have also enacted "fetal pain" laws restricting abortions after twenty weeks, when it is thought that fetuses have developed the ability to feel pain (though some doctors argue that capacity begins even as early as eight-and-a-half weeks). In at least one other state, there has been a movement to ban abortions after the detection of a fetal heartbeat, at about six to ten weeks' gestation.

The "viability," "fetal pain," and "fetal heartbeat" arguments show that even where abortion laws are permissive, a woman's "right" to abort the child in her womb is curtailed by what is, in effect, a recognition of the humanity of the unborn child. "A woman's right to choose" has never been seen, even in those states, as an absolute or unconditional right. In most cases, the law accepts that unborn life has rights, but is unable to agree on the point at which those rights can be asserted at the expense of other rights. The use of "viability," "fetal pain," and "fetal heartbeat" as "scientific" ways of determining the limits of a woman's right is a way of keeping the peace in a society divided over the issue. What the science actually says is, of course, disputed, and harnessed to political and ethical views; what the science indisputably reveals, on the other hand, is what we already knew — that the life in the womb is deeply, marvelously human.

There are also other sorts of "common-sense" restrictions that take into account the need for an informed decision for women, especially minors. A host of legislation in recent years has introduced such measures as mandated counseling, ultrasounds, and parental notification and/ or consent. According to the (pro-choice) Guttmacher Institute, 2011 was a record year: "The 80 abortion restrictions enacted this year is more than double the previous record of 34 abortion restrictions enacted in 2005, and more than triple the 23 enacted in 2010."

The bishops favor (and are) working for just these sorts of step-by-step restrictions to abortion, which both reflect and effect greater cultural appreciation for the dignity and value of all human life.

Months before he was named to head the Philadelphia archdiocese, Denver's Archbishop Charles J. Chaput gave a talk to a group of Catholic laity emphasizing that renewing a culture of life is the "ultimate goal":

> Culture is everything. Culture is our "human ecology." It's the environment where we human beings breathe not only air, but ideas, beliefs, and values. Getting political influence has obvious and important short-term value. But it's not what pro-lifers are finally about. Our real task, and our much longer-term and more important goal, is to carry out what John Paul II called the "evangelization of culture."
>
> *We need to work to change the culture.* That demands a life-long commitment to education, Christian formation, and, ultimately, conversion. Only saints really change the world. And therein lies our ultimate victory: If we change one heart at a time, while we save one unborn life at a time, the day will come when we won't need to worry about saving babies, because they'll be surrounded by a loving and welcoming culture.
>
> Will I see that day with my own eyes? I don't think I can hold my breath that long. But then, I never expected to see a Polish pope or the fall of the Iron Curtain either. We may or may not see that day in our own lifetimes, but the children of your grandchildren *will see that day.* The future depends on our choices and actions right here, right now, today — together.

Even among staunch abortion activists, there is evidence that pro-life witness has forced a change of strategy, if not completely of hearts. In a controversial *Washington Post* op-ed piece that some pro-choice advocates described as a "sellout," Frances Kissling, former president of Catholics for Choice wrote:

> The fetus is more visible than ever before, and the abortion-rights movement needs to accept its existence and its value. It may not have a right to life, and its value may not be equal to

that of the pregnant woman, but ending the life of a fetus is not a morally insignificant event. Very few people would argue that there is no difference between the decision to abort at 6 weeks and the decision to do so when the fetus would be viable outside of the womb, which today is generally at 24 to 26 weeks. Still, it is rare for mainstream movement leaders to say that publicly. Abortion is not merely a medical matter, and there is an unintended coarseness to claiming that it is.

We need to firmly and clearly reject post-viability abortions except in extreme cases. Exceptions include when the woman's life is at immediate risk; when the fetus suffers from conditions that are incompatible with a good quality of life; or when the woman's health is seriously threatened by a medical or psychological condition that continued pregnancy will exacerbate. We should regulate post-viability abortion to include the confirmation of those conditions by medical or psychiatric specialists.

Those kinds of regulations are not anti-woman or unduly invasive. They rightly protect all of our interests in women's health and fetal life.

Kissling was not rolling back on her support for abortion. But her willingness to back away from the "twin absolutes of choice or life" shows a gradual shift of position from which pro-lifers can take heart — and a lesson: that the tide is turning in favor of the unborn.

Embryo Research

In the arguments over federal funding for embryonic stem-cell research that began in the mid-1990s it was repeatedly claimed that the creation and cloning of human embryos (creating human-animal hybrids) would enable cures for Alzheimer's, Parkinson's, and other diseases. Those who opposed the legalization of this new development in the disrespect of human life were depicted as religious fanatics putting obstacles in the path of medical progress. Science, we were told, needed the greatest freedom for success; and the United States, already the world leader in stem-cell research, needed a law that would unfetter its research laboratories and so help usher in a new generation of seemingly astonishing cures.

For sufferers of those ailments, this was irresponsible hype and a cruel deception. Embryonic stem-cell research has resulted in no significant medical developments. There are no treatments derived from embryonic stem cells. On the other hand, there are literally dozens of treatments involving adult stem cells (extracted from bone marrow or placentas), which are entirely ethical. Stem-cell science is indeed at the cutting edge of medical research; there have been huge strides made in creating new organs from stem cells. Yet none of these has involved *embryonic* stem cells.

The demand for embryonic research comes from private medical research companies seeking funding. To attract backers, they need constantly to dangle the possibility of breakthroughs as result of cutting-edge, blue-sky experiments. Their interest is in expanding the possibilities of what they can do in the laboratory in the hope that at some point an unforeseen development will occur. They have lobbied hard for the freedom to explore all options so that *at the end of the road* miracle cures will be available. Privately, scientists say the arguments of the lobby are highly questionable, but are afraid to speak out because their institutions would lose the huge grants on which they depend.

Other countries take the protection of the embryo far more seriously, and view what is taking place in Asia, the United States, and the United Kingdom with alarm. Following the 2008 passage in Britain of the Human Fertilization and Embryology Act, allowing the laboratory creation and cloning of human embryos, a number of countries in Europe expressed strong reservations about the way the need to weigh ethical reservations about the use of human life against the anticipated benefits of research had been simply ignored. The German Medical Association, for example, expressed concern that the British were "developing a completely different relationship to growing life."

The huge expansion of public funding for human embryonic stem-cell research in the United States — estimated by the National Institutes of Health to be $128 million in 2011 — marked the triumph of a deeply troubling dogma: that scientific enquiry should be unfettered. This dogma replaces an important traditional principle: that tampering with human life for medical purposes requires a compelling ethical justification.

The ethical duty society owes to human life requires a stringent scrutiny of claims of possible benefits. This ethical calculus — a reasoned examination of the ethics weighed against the anticipated benefits — conflicts with the medical-research lobby's unreasonable claim to be free of any such calculus. Good science has always been accompanied by ethical standards. Ethics is good for science. Standards and trust are key.

It suits the advocates of embryonic research to frame its opponents as religious fanatics opposing the freedom of scientific enquiry ("remember Galileo!"). But the ethical calculus is not a religious idea; advocates of good science have always upheld it as a vital principle. If the ends always justified the means, there can be no objection to the kind of experiments carried out by Nazi scientists on human beings.

Catholics are sometimes asked by sufferers of terminal diseases what they have to say to them. "How can you sit there and oppose what could make me better?" The answer is that those who have those diseases have been sold a lie. Adult stem-cell research is far more likely to produce a cure for them. The newspapers may be talking about breakthroughs from embryonic research, but the scientific journals are not.

Yet it is not because embryonic research has failed to produce the much-hyped cures that it is wrong. A human embryo is the first stage of life; to use human life as the subject of experimentation is to desecrate that life. The fact that researchers use embryos left over from IVF treatment, which would be destroyed anyway, in no way distracts from the essential wrongness of experimenting on human life.

Few would maintain the cluster of cells that makes up an embryo is morally equivalent to other clusters of cells — cancerous cells, say, or the embryo of a rat. If the embryo were so regarded, there would not have been such debate within the Presidential Commission for the Study of Bioethical Issues on whether funding should be expanded or not.

Nor is this a matter of Catholics seeking to "impose" their religious views about embryos on broader society. Father Tad Pacholczyk, a bioethicist who earned a doctorate in neuroscience at Yale and did post-graduate research at Harvard Medical School before entering the seminary, calls the "religious imposition" argument illogical and simply a rhetorical ploy. In one of his weekly bioethics columns, he writes this about an experience he had after participating in Virginia legislative hearings on embryonic stem-cell research:

During my testimony, I pointed out how in the United States we have stringent federal laws that protect not only the national bird, the bald eagle, but also that eagle's eggs. If you were to chance upon some of them in a nest out in the wilderness, it would be illegal for you to destroy those eggs. By the force of law, we recognize how the egg of the bald eagle, that is to say, the embryonic eagle inside that egg, is the same creature as the glorious bird that we witness flying high overhead. Therefore, we pass laws to safeguard not only the adult but also the very youngest member of that species. Even atheists can see how a bald eagle's eggs should be protected; it's really not a religious question at all. What's so troublesome is how we are able to understand the importance of protecting the earliest stages of animal life, but when it comes to our own human life, a kind of mental disconnect takes place. Our moral judgment quickly becomes murky and obtuse when we desire to do certain things that are not good, like having abortions, or destroying embryonic humans for their stem cells.

So anytime we come across a lawmaker who tries to suggest that an argument in defense of sound morals is nothing but imposing a religious viewpoint, we need to look deeper at what may really be taking place. That lawmaker may not be so concerned about avoiding the imposition of a particular view on others — more likely, they are jockeying to simply be able to impose their view, a view which is ultimately much less tenable and defensible in terms of sound moral thinking. Hence they seek to short-circuit the discussion by stressing religious zealotry and imposition without ever confronting the substantive ethical or bioethical argument itself. Once the religious imposition card is played, and Christian lawmakers suddenly become weak-kneed about defending human life and sound morals, the other side then feels free to do the imposing themselves, without having expended too much effort on confronting the essence of the moral debate itself.

Surplus Embryos

In vitro fertilization (IVF) creates many surplus embryos, which are then frozen or destroyed, or used for medical experiments. Inherent in the technique is selecting an embryo for implantation in the womb. This power has led, inevitably, to calls to allow embryos to be selected (or screened) for particular characteristics: gender, hair color, and so on. We are back, once more, to eugenics.

This call strikes at the heart of one of the core moral principles undergirding a civilized society — that you don't use anyone else just for your own purposes, or even for other people's purposes. A human person needs to be treated as an end in himself or herself, not a tool for someone else's agenda. It is on this basis that we condemn rape, torture, and blackmail; that we don't allow experiments on people's bodies or minds without their consent; and that we don't breed human individuals to create a pool of organs that could be transplanted to save the lives of others.

That is why "savior siblings" and other forms of embryo selection are wrong. Using a technique known as pre-implantation genetic diagnosis (PGD), certain embryos created through IVF are chosen (and others rejected) because they contain a particularly desirable gene or genes — eye color, gender, etc. A savior sibling is a child brought into the world in order to provide an organ or cell transplant to a brother or sister who is affected with a rare fatal blood disease. Couples using IVF can pick and choose from the embryos available to them until they find one that will grow into a baby whose marrow is a genetic fit. These children may be loved by their parents, but they have been born in order to be donors, to be used by another human being. God made us ends, not means. The Vatican instruction *Dignitas personae* (on the dignity of the person) deplores the eugenic mentality behind embryo selection:

> Pre-implantation diagnosis — connected as it is with artificial fertilization, which is itself always intrinsically illicit — is directed toward the *qualitative selection and consequent destruction of embryos,* which constitutes an act of abortion. Pre-implantation diagnosis is therefore the expression of a *eugenic mentality* that accepts selective abortion in order to prevent the birth of children affected by various types of anomalies. Such an attitude is shameful and utterly reprehensible, since it presumes to meas-

ure the value of a human life only within the parameters of "normality" and physical well-being, thus opening the way to legitimizing infanticide and euthanasia as well.

Ⳅ

EXISTING FRAME

"Most people in this country believe the right to an abortion should be enshrined in law. If the Church had its way, there would be a return to the back-street abortion.

"Research on embryos that are just a cluster of cells and not viable gives the hope of finding a cure for terrible diseases. How is it wrong to have a second child (a so-called savior sibling) who can give stem cells to save their brother or sister?"

REFRAME

The Catholic Church speaks on behalf of the voiceless, defenseless embryo, just as it speaks on behalf of other "silent" victims. The Church seeks to bring down the upper legal limit on abortion in order to reach a point where abortion is no longer practiced. At the same time, the Church seeks to promote public awareness of the fragility and value of unborn life and to offer real choices to women frightened by unplanned or unwanted pregnancies. The Church wants to work toward creating a society where all life is welcomed and valued.

Embryos are the early stage of human life; they are vulnerable and need protection from the law. The real good news is the rapid progress made in adult stem-cell research. All the major developments have been in adult stem cells, not embryonic ones. Claims made for embryonic stem-cell research are exaggerated and wishful — the result of hype by corporations and research labs seeking publicity and funding.

Ⳅ

Key Messages

- The Catholic Church is a major investor in adult stem-cell research — Vatican labs, Catholic hospitals, etc.
- All science is governed by an ethical framework — good science and good ethics go together (embryonic stem-cell research has been marred by scandals: it is dangerous).

- There are powerful corporate interests behind embryonic stem-cell research. Unborn life is a powerless plaything in the hands of those interests.
- Embryos are the early stage of human life; they are vulnerable and need protection from the law.
- The worth of human life is not linked to its appearance or size — because an embryo is tiny makes it no less a human life, or unworthy of care and protection.
- The United States has a casual attitude toward embryos, compared with leading European countries, which are much more strictly regulated. Disrespect for embryos signals a wider disrespect for human life, which is morally corrosive.
- There is a moral awakening in American society — a growing awareness of the wonder and beauty of unborn life. The Catholic Church speaks on behalf of the voiceless, defenseless embryo, just as it speaks on behalf of other "silent" victims.
- The Church supports incremental restrictions on abortion in order to reach a point where abortion is no longer practiced.
- At the same time, the Church seeks to promote public awareness of the fragility and value of unborn life and to offer real choices to women frightened by unplanned or unwanted pregnancies.
- The Church wants to work toward creating a society where all life is welcomed and valued. This is not a matter of the rights of women versus other rights. There are others involved — men and the unborn life. The rights of women are best protected by ensuring that pregnant women are supported in every way possible.

Chapter 7

Catholics and AIDS

— Challenging Questions —

- *Why doesn't the Church recognize that effective use of condoms would save millions of lives in Africa?*
- *When many men working away from home are infected by prostitutes and then infect their wives when they go home, how can the Church forbid the use of condoms?*
- *Shouldn't prostitutes and others not ready to embrace chastity be encouraged to use condoms?*
- *Has the Pope recently backtracked on the Church's absolute ban on condoms?*

The world may be adept at ignoring the plight of Africa, but no one can ignore the HIV/AIDS pandemic, the greatest threat to that continent since the slave trade. It seems obvious to most people in Western countries that, just as the widespread use of condoms contributed to bringing down rates of HIV transmission among gay men in the United States and Western Europe in the 1980s, the "answer" to AIDS in Africa must be more of the same. Yet HIV (the virus that causes AIDS) in Africa has different characteristics, and a deluge of evidence points to the ineffectiveness of campaigns encouraging people to have "safe sex."

The Church's alternative policy — encouraging responsible sexual behavior, while tackling the stigma of AIDS and poverty — is born not just of moral conviction but of knowledge of the realities of Africa on the ground. To the secular Western mind, however, it seems just the opposite: the imposition by detached dogmatists of a religious doctrine. As a result, Catholics find themselves admonished for "contributing to the spread of the virus," "sacrificing innocent lives on the altar of dogma., and even "being directly responsible for the deaths of millions of Africans."

We have therefore a large task of reframing. But once the facts are examined, it is clear that it is the "more condoms" approach which betrays a detached, even colonialist, mentality; abstinence programs, on the other hand, have a proven track record of success in curbing the spread of the virus. As is now finally being accepted, the early strategy of the UNAIDS program was based on a fatal misreading of African realities; the approach which had worked so well in the 1980s in Europe and the United States, it turned out, was quite inappropriate for Africa, while precisely those programs which aimed at behavior change have proved to be the most successful — the kind of programs which the Catholic Church (among others) had argued were the key to defeating AIDS.

In his 2003 book *Rethinking AIDS Prevention*, the anthropologist and Harvard expert Edward C. Green attributes this disaster to the mind-set of the mainly European and American health experts who advise governments on their policies for combating AIDS. Many of to-day's international health bureaucracies were established in the 1970s, when the governments of rich countries, fearing population explosion in poor countries, poured money into programs to promote contraception. When AIDS began to spread in the 1980s, therefore, it was easy to deploy these same methods to combat the virus — especially as condoms had proved effective in reducing AIDS among promiscuous groups in the United States and Europe. But the causes of the rapid spread of African AIDS were very different, as we shall see.

The Church argued against those flawed strategies from the start. No other organization has had such intense involvement on the frontline of prevention and treatment in sub-Saharan Africa and other developing countries; no single civil-society organization can match the Church's presence and activity in both the prevention and treatment of HIV among the poor, and especially among the most remote villages and in the poorest slums. That pervasive presence hardly makes it "detached" from the realities in Africa, as some critics have held. Other critics agree that the Catholic presence and influence are enormous, but use that fact to blame the Church for failing to include condoms as part of its HIV-prevention strategy. But this criticism wrongly assumes that condoms are the key to combating AIDS in Africa.

The question turns, therefore, on the "effectiveness" of condoms in combating HIV. There is plenty of hard evidence that condoms-based campaigns against HIV in sub-Saharan Africa, where 22.5 million people are infected (about two-thirds of the world's total), have failed to contain the spread of the virus, for reasons we will come to; and in most cases, the evidence shows, have aggravated it. However, it is also true that the use of condoms has been effective — although not as effective as partner reduction — in reducing transmission among particular high-risk sub-groups, notably prostitutes. In this sense, therefore, neither the statement "condoms are effective in reducing HIV transmission" nor "'condoms are ineffective in reducing HIV transmission" is per se true. What the science shows is that, in the African population at large, behavior change is the key factor in reducing virus transmission; and by encouraging risky behavior, condom campaigns cause transmission rates to increase. On the other hand, among groups engaging in highly risky behavior who are not ready or willing to change, condoms may cause transmission rates to decrease. But this is a very small population compared with the first.

To add to the confusion, there have been concerns raised by some African bishops in the past — and even, at one stage, by a Vatican cardinal — that condoms are "porous" and do not, in fact, act as a barrier to the transmission of the virus. These claims are not supported by the evidence; the paper which attempted to present that case, published in 2004 by Cardinal Alfonso López Trujillo, then head of the Council for the Family at the Vatican, was widely derided, and has been allowed to quietly drop. Because the paper received extensive media treatment, however, when Church leaders — including, notably, Pope Benedict in 2009 — assert the ineffectiveness of condoms-based strategies against HIV in the wider population, they are often wrongly heard as claiming that condoms are porous, and met with derision. But as Pope Benedict knew very well, condoms have proved ineffective against AIDS in Africa, but not because they are "porous."

The key assumption that hounds this discussion, and the flaw in the strategy of the international agencies up until relatively recently, is the persistent myth that what worked to bring down HIV rates in Europe and the United States — namely, widespread condom use within the most vulnerable population, gay men — will also bring it down in Africa, where HIV is spread mainly through heterosexual intercourse.

But after two decades, the failure of this "technical" strategy is clear: HIV transmission rates in Africa soared between 1990 and 2005, as international organizations pumped billions into promoting condom use. On the other hand, the Church's assertion that AIDS will be defeated only by behavior change, and by addressing the conditions which make AIDS in Africa different from developed Northern countries, now looks, on the basis purely of the evidence, to be the far stronger case.

The controversy has been fueled by warm discussions among moral theologians and Church leaders on the narrower question of whether, in the case of people unready or unable to embrace monogamy, fidelity, and abstinence, it is incumbent upon the Church to urge them to use condoms as prophylactics, where the intention is to prevent death rather than life. Pope Benedict intervened in this discussion in November 2010. In *Light of the World* he cited the case of a prostitute who chooses to use a condom in order to avoid infecting someone, and interpreted this act of care as the possible beginning of a journey of moral awakening. The pope's few lines in the interview were later clarified in a statement from the Congregation for the Doctrine of the Faith, which allows us now to state the Church's position with greater precision.

଼

Positive Intention

Millions of people are in danger of being infected in Africa and sooner or later dying of AIDS. Children are being left orphaned, migrant workers are having sex with infected prostitutes, and then coming home and infecting their wives. Many of these lives could be saved by using condoms. So the Church seems both distant and heartless when it says that condom use is not the solution but part of the problem, and dogmatic to suggest that abstinence and fidelity are better solutions. The Church should be willing to accept condom use, even at the risk of condoning adultery, fornication, incest, and other abuses, or apparently violating Church teaching against artificial contraception within marriage. Is it not better to prefer "to save lives" than to sacrifice them in order to defend its teaching? The value behind this criticism of the Church's position is one that Christians should recognize from the Gospels.

଼

"The Church Has AIDS"

Helen Epstein, a Jewish-American journalist and author of a highly praised 2007 book on the virus, *The Invisible Cure*, notes that "Catholic and Protestant churches had been running exemplary AIDS programs in Africa since the 1980s." No organization has been closer to, and more involved with, the communities afflicted by AIDS than the Catholic Church. And no organization has been more effective in tackling AIDS at its root.

Along with Protestant churches, Catholics were on the "front lines" as soon as the epidemic began, responding to the imperative to care for the suffering and dying and to educate the human family in ways to prevent the further spread of HIV. Today, often in partnership with others, they play a vital and expanding role in the comprehensive response to HIV across the developing world: assisting people in avoiding infection; providing tests to find out if people are infected and offering physical and spiritual care to those who are; working in communities to combat stigmatization and discrimination; caring for those affected (especially widows and orphans); helping those infected to "live positively"; and advocating on behalf of persons living with HIV or AIDS. This large-scale service of a suffering population has given rise to theological reflection. So closely do Catholics identify with those infected that some speak of the Church itself "living with AIDS."

Catholic AIDS programs work through existing diocesan/parish structures; they do not come from "outside," but are part of the Church's everyday mission, which is why they are valued by international agencies for both their compassion and effectiveness. The Church is not merely a nongovernmental organization providing a service for the people; the Church *is* the people. Bishop Kevin Dowling of Rustenberg, former chair of the Southern African Catholic Bishops' Conference's (SACBC) AIDS office, puts it this way: The Church's response "is intimately linked to its mission in the world, a response which must be based on and reveal fundamental Gospel attitudes, values, such as compassion, solidarity, care for the vulnerable, striving for justice, and commitment to overcoming unjust structures in society." Bishop Dowling goes on to list the practical actions which flow from this:

> We stand with, we want to be with the little ones, the people who do not count, who will never be listened to because they are not given access to anything or any structure; those who are lost in some outlying community or urban slum which will

rarely, if ever, be visited by anyone; the little ones who end up simply being a number, a statistic, whether it be in terms of the escalating infection rate or in terms of the escalating numbers of dead in the mortuaries awaiting a pauper's funeral, sometimes for months on end because families cannot be traced. We want to be with the poorest and alienated communities, to be present to and involved with them in their reality.

Leaving aside its many other qualifications to speak on this issue, therefore, the number and reach of its programs mean the Church deserves to be recognized as possibly the world's leading voice on AIDS. Yet consistently it has been sidelined from the debate over the international community's response to the virus because of its "dogmatic" opposition to contraception — an irony, given what we now know about the international agencies' dogmatic opposition to behavior-change strategies.

According to UNAIDS (2010) about 22.5 million sub-Saharan Africans are infected, nearly 70 percent of the total global population of 33.3 million living with HIV. Between 2000 and 2020, about 55 million Africans will have died of AIDS-related diseases. The pandemic has decimated the people of the area, wiping out, in many areas, half of the working-age population, leaving grandparents to care for their orphaned grandchildren. Vatican officials estimate that around the world the Church ministers to more than 25 percent of all those with HIV/AIDS. In Africa, that figure rises to 50 to 75 percent, and in many remote areas, close to 100 percent.

The Southern African bishops' AIDS Office, founded in 2000, coordinates more than 150 programs in the region which prevent and treat AIDS. It runs a vast network of hospitals, clinics, hospices, home-based care projects, and orphanages, and has pioneered programs for women and young people to educate and enable them to resist sexual advances. Literally hundreds of thousands of people in South Africa, Namibia, Swaziland, Botswana, and Lesotho have received training and support from Catholic programs. Dozens of Catholic schools teach HIV prevention in their curricula.

Given that half of new HIV infections are found among the 15-to-24-year-old age group, the SACBC AIDS Office has focused on young adults in particular. Its programs develop attitudes of commitment and responsibility in sexual behavior, making young people aware of the unequal power relationship between men and women and ways in which they can promote and advance their equal dignity. Its three other priorities are: 1) community-based care for the sick and dying, and care for orphans; 2) programs of education and awareness that tackle the silence and the stigma attached to HIV, encouraging people to be tested and to talk about the virus; and 3) combating the poverty and ignorance which often lie at the root of the spread of HIV.

Why are so many young people infected? The AIDS Office identifies the following reasons:

1.   migrant labor, and the fragmentation of families;
2.   extreme poverty, which forces young women into the sex trade;
3.   vulnerable teenagers, orphaned by parents dying in large numbers from AIDS, made to have sex with relatives; and
4.   the bombardment of young people with the message — sponsored by international organizations — that it is fine to have sex, as long as they do it "safely."

The AIDS Office's chief prevention program for young people is called "Education for Life." Originally developed by Catholics in Uganda, where it is credited with significantly reducing the rate of new infections there, it stresses long-term abstinence and lifelong and mutual fidelity among spouses. The program is summed up as "ABCD". "Abstain, Be faithful, Change your lifestyle, or you are in Danger of contracting HIV."

Another key element of the prevention program is the testing of pregnant mothers and the use of antiretroviral drugs to prevent mother-to-baby transmission. The Catholic Church is exceptional in southern Africa in the extent of its provision to the sick and the dying. Its network of hospices has expanded to meet the vast demand from people living with AIDS. Its clinics offer nutrition and antiretroviral treatment.

The AIDS Office also is involved in advocating legal reform on issues related to people living with or affected by HIV, particularly with regard to children's rights; in advocating for free education for orphans and disability grants for the sick; and in expanding access to antiretroviral drugs. Its projects seek to overcome stigma and prejudice toward people living with or affected by HIV within parishes.

In short, the Catholic Church in southern Africa has the infrastructure, the passion, the resources, the expertise, the experience, and the dedication to confront the challenge of AIDS. Its prevention programs are highly effective in educating young people to resist sexual advances, and to abstain until marriage. A large part of the effectiveness of the Church's anti-HIV programs lies in their community-based approach, depending on a large network of volunteers with strong values and a dedication to helping others.

The (In)Effectiveness of Condoms-Based Campaigns

Condom use is only effective in reducing HIV transmission within identifiable subgroups (prostitutes, gay men), not in the population at large, where it has the opposite effect: evidence correlates the greater availability and use of condoms with higher infection rates. There are many reasons for this, not least the idea of risk compensation implicit in the idea of "safe" sex. Just as, in the West, the removal of the fear of unwanted pregnancies through widespread contraception has led to the age of first sexual encounter becoming lower year after year, so in Africa condoms campaigns have sent the message to young people that it's okay to have sex. This "risk compensation," or "behavioral disinhibition," is what has fueled the spread of the virus, according to one of the world's leading experts on AIDS, Dr. Edward C. Green of Harvard University. "People take more sexual risks," he says, "because they feel safer than is actually justified when using condoms."

Another reason is that condom use is simply not consistent or prevalent enough, in spite of massive promotions, to reduce the virus — a consequence of poor infrastructure and transportation networks and other aspects of poverty. In a May 9, 2008, article for *Science* magazine, ten AIDS experts concluded that "consistent condom use has not reached a sufficiently high level, even after many years of widespread and often aggressive promotion, to produce a measurable slowing of the new infections in the generalized epidemics of sub-Saharan Africa." The biggest chunk of the $3.2 billion UNAIDS budget has been allocated to condoms-based interventions which are "unsupported by rigorous evidence," they add, noting that only 20 percent has been directed at generalized epidemics in Africa, and a negligible part of that budget has been directed at changing sexual behavior.

Those same experts emphasize that "partner reduction" is the key to curbing AIDS. The reason this strategy is so dramatically effective is not as obvious as it might appear. Epstein's study, *The Invisible Cure*, showed how "concurrency" — having multiple, long-term sexual partners — was the key reason why HIV rates were increasing despite increased condom use. Although the evidence for this was everywhere, the reluctance to translate it into international policies aimed at partner reduction, as Epstein's book devastatingly shows, has everything to do with a reluctance on the part of Western liberals to introduce programs of moral behavior that would challenge their own values.

"Concurrency" is the name given to a particularly African form of infidelity.

In Europe and the United States, promiscuity is associated with casual sex (one-night stands and uncommitted relationships); in Africa, however, the main vehicle for the rapid escalation of the virus has been the prevalence of committed, long-term multiple relationships, which act as a kind of "superhighway" for the virus. As Epstein puts it: "AIDS is common in Africa not because African people have so many sexual partners, but because they are more likely than people in other world regions to have a small number of concurrent long-term partners. This places them, along with their partner or partners, within a vast network of ongoing sexual relationships that is highly conducive to the spread of HIV."

She argues that there are many other, interlocking and multifaceted, reasons for the prevalence of concurrency: the imbalance of power between genders, war and instability, forced migration, alcohol, abuse, and pervasive violence, all of which cause the poor in Africa to seek protection in long-term sexual relationships.

The key factor in the spread of AIDS in Africa, therefore, is a particular form of promiscuity. Although Africans are not more promiscuous (in the Western sense) than people in Europe and the United States, concurrency is widespread.

While condoms are effective in reducing the spread of the virus in casual sexual encounters, they are seldom used in long-term, stable relationships, which is where most of the AIDS transmission in Africa occurs. That is why, although partner reduction has played a key role in reducing HIV rates all over the world, in Africa the effect has been especially dramatic. In Zimbabwe and Kenya, for example, the HIV rate began to decline in the late 1990s as numbers of multiple partnerships fell; but in Botswana, South Africa, and Lesotho, where no partner reduction occurred in the 1990s, and where condoms were emphasized as the main method of prevention, HIV rates soared.

Why have international organizations been so slow to recognize this, and to urge sexual behavior change? Until 2006 no public health program in southern Africa informed people of the dangers of concurrency, and the topic was absent from the policy documents of every international public health organization. Instead, the "fixation" — as the pope calls it — on the technical solution of condoms has been driven "not by evidence but by ideology, stereotypes, and false assumptions," according to Dr. Green. That ideology had everything to do with UN-AIDS officials moving into AIDS from family planning, where the notion of a policy based on morality was anathema. (At the 2005 international AIDS conference in Bangkok, researchers presenting evidence about the importance of fidelity in AIDS prevention were accused of "moralizing" and "practically booed off stage," records Epstein.)

Edward Green, himself an agnostic scientist, was one of a handful of experts who for years had been arguing that faithfulness was key to combating the virus. Sidelined and ignored in the 1990s, these experts now represent mainstream scientific opinion, although the Western media, reflecting ignorance of the evidence in wider society, has been slow to catch on: hence the hailstorm of outrage which met Benedict XVI when, on his way to Cameroon in March 2009, he told journalists that AIDS is "a tragedy that cannot be overcome by money alone, and that cannot be overcome by the distribution of condoms, which even aggravates the problems."

Dr. Green, the author of five books and 250 peer-reviewed articles, said the Pope was "actually correct." Condoms-based campaigns, he said, "result in efforts that are at best ineffective and at worst harmful."

Another "lone voice," James Shelton of the U.S. Agency for International Development, also agreed with Pope Benedict; as he wrote in the *Lancet,* "condoms alone have limited impact in generalized epidemics." And indeed, no country in Africa has yet turned back a generalized epidemic by means of condom distribution. In Cameroon, to where the pope was traveling when he made his remarks, between 1992 and 2001 condom sales increased from 6 million to 15 million, while HIV-infection rates tripled, from 3 percent to 9 percent.

As Father Michael Czerny, former director of the African Jesuit AIDS Network (AJAN) puts it: "The promotion of condoms as the strategy for reducing HIV infection in a general population is based on statistical probability and intuitive plausibility. It enjoys considerable credibility in the Western media and among Western opinion makers. What it lacks is scientific support."

Condoms-based campaigns carry an implicit pessimism about human beings, seeing people as rapacious, unable to control themselves, and incapable of moving beyond self-gratification. It is also an attitude alien to traditional African values. Imposed by international agencies on Africans, it represents, says Father Czerny, an "unconscious racism."

The Other Approach

The Church's approach, gained from experience on the ground among some of the poorest communities in Africa blighted by AIDS, is that the virus must be tackled in two key ways.

The first is through the "humanization of sexuality," based on faith in God and respect for oneself and others, in contrast to the "banalization of sexuality" implicit in condom campaigns. Sound epidemiological research supports the Church's approach. As Dr. Green writes: "As evidence mounts about the high prevalence and deadly nature of multiple and concurrent partnerships, we must reorient prevention interventions and research to promote behavior change — in particular, partner reduction and sexual exclusivity." The classic example is Uganda, where HIV prevalence declined from 21 percent to 9.8 percent in the 1990s following a reduction in non-regular sexual partners by 65 percent. That shift in behavior was the result of a government-backed, community-based campaign supported by the churches.

The campaign did not exclude condoms, but it was behavior change — according to a 2004 report in the journal *Science* by authors Rand L. Stoneburner and Daniel Low-Beer — which was the crucial factor. "There were a wide range of sexual behavior changes in Uganda: reducing partners, abstinence, faithfulness, marriage, increased condom use, as well as others we probably will never know about," they write. "The major difference in Uganda is a reduction in non-regular sexual partners and an associated contraction of sexual networks."

In July 2010 UNAIDS announced significant reductions in rates of transmission among young people as the result of behavior change. According to a Reuters report, "the study found the main drivers of the reductions were changes in sexual behavior. Young people in 13 of the 25 countries were waiting longer before they become sexually active. In more than half of the 25 countries, young people were choosing to have fewer sexual partners."

This approach is the most effective, the most realistic, and the most successful. Nor is there an alternative. As the Catholic bishops of Africa put it in their message at the end of the Second Synod of Bishops for Africa (October 2009): "The problem cannot be overcome by the distribution of prophylactics. We appeal to all who are genuinely interested in arresting the sexual transmission of HIV to recognize the success of programs that propose abstinence among those not yet married, and fidelity among the married. Such a course not only offers the best protection against the spread of this disease, but is also in harmony with Christian morality."

The second part of the Church's approach is described by Pope Benedict in *Light of the World* as assisting people "up close and concretely" through "prevention, education, help, counsel, and accompaniment." People can change their behavior only with support from those who are willing to come alongside them, offering solace and assistance. Despair is the enemy of change. Faith is its friend. A Church which tirelessly serves those in need is credible in the teaching and formation it offers.

High-Risk Groups and Condoms: What Does the Church Say?

Because of the large numbers of Catholics living with AIDS, and because the Church's outreach to the infected excludes no one, the Church has been faced over the years with the ethical question of whether it is up to the Church to give information about the use of condoms to people engaging in high-risk sexual behavior who are unable or not ready to change that behavior.

Distributing condoms is out of the question: that would be to exacerbate the problem already outlined, and undermine the Church's message. (As Pope Benedict says in *Light of the World*, "People can get condoms when they want anyway.") The question has been whether Catholic pastoral practice can include urging a man or woman who is infected or engaging in high-risk sexual behavior to protect themselves or others. Some maintain that this would be to condone harmful and sinful behavior, and/or advocate artificial contraception, which is forbidden in *Humanae Vitae*; others that the prophylactic use of condoms falls outside *Humanae Vitae,* which is concerned with marital love, and especially the virtue of chastity within marriage. Condoms, in this reading, are things, not evil in themselves; what makes them wrong is the use to which they are put; and if their purpose is prophylactic rather than contraceptive, and the purpose is to prevent infection, their use may be justified.

In *Light of the World*, Pope Benedict introduces a pastoral viewpoint, recognizing that, in the case of a prostitute using a condom, this could be "a first step in the direction of a moralization, a first assumption of responsibility, on the way to recovering an awareness that not everything is allowed and one cannot do whatever one wants." But he went on to repeat that condom use was neither a real nor a moral solution to AIDS, which requires a "humanization of sexuality." Yet if the person recognizes the other's vulnerability, and so a certain responsibility to take care to avoid infection, this could be "a first step" down that road.

The Congregation for the Doctrine of the Faith (CDF) subsequently clarified Benedict XVI's remarks. The pope was:

a. not altering or departing from either the moral teaching or the pastoral practice of the Church;
b. not referring to a case relevant to the Church's teaching on conjugal love in *Humanae Vitae* (in other words, this did not alter the doctrine on contraception);
c. not claiming that condoms are in any sense the right or moral response to AIDS;
d. not endorsing the principle of lesser evil, which is vulnerable to the error of proportionalism; and
e. not claiming that the use of a condom by an HIV-infected prostitute diminishes the evil of prostitution.

What the pope *was* saying — "in full conformity with the moral theological tradition of the Church" — was that those who engage in promiscuous behavior knowing themselves to be an HIV-infected risk are sinning against the Fifth Commandment (thou shall not kill) as well as against the Sixth (thou shall not commit adultery), and that therefore "anyone who uses a condom in order to diminish the risk posed to another person is intending to reduce the evil connected with his or her immoral activity." The CDF added that "those involved in prostitution who are HIV positive and who seek to diminish the risk of contagion by the use of a condom may be taking the first step in respecting the life of another — even if the evil of prostitution remains in all its gravity."

Summarizing these often complex ideas simply, we can say: The Church urges HIV-infected and sexually promiscuous people to abstain and be faithful. The Church does not urge the use of condoms, which overall aggravate the problem. But in the extreme case of prostitutes who are unwilling or, practically speaking, unable to abstain, their intention to use a condom to reduce the risk of infection may be a step in the direction of taking responsibility.

Another case often raised is that of the "sero-discordant" married couple, where one spouse is infected and the other is not, or where both are HIV-infected. The CDF's clarification pointed out that the pope's remarks in *Light of the World* did not address that question, so it would be pointless to extrapolate. It is, however, obvious that in this situation a very strong risk of infection exists. The HIV-positive partner is very likely to infect the other; a doubly infected couple is likely to exacerbate the destruction of their respective immune systems by "re-infecting" each other with different strains of the virus. Abstinence, therefore, is the path of greatest responsibility. According to the Second Special Session for Africa of the Synod of Bishops, the Church offers "a pastoral support which helps couples living with an infected spouse to inform and form their consciences, so that they might choose what is right, with full responsibility for the greater good of each other, their union and their family."

❧

EXISTING FRAME

"The Church is more concerned with its outdated views on sex than it is in saving lives in Africa. If people were taught to use condoms properly, millions of lives could be saved. The Church is heartless in its pursuit of principles over care of the sick and dying."

REFRAME

The Church is the leading and often sole provider of care to those sick and dying of AIDS in Africa. No organization knows and understands AIDS better. The Church's programs do not just propose that which is morally right, but also that which works best: behavior change. The evidence supports this approach; among populations at large, campaigns of condom promotion have exacerbated the problem. The Church's message seems countercultural but is epidemiologically the soundest option.

As Pope Benedict has made clear, among people engaging in high-risk behavior, the Church continues to propose abstinence or fidelity. If such people choose to use a condom in order to protect another from infection, this may well be a step in the moral direction. This is not a change in teaching on contraception.

☃

Key Messages

- When the Church speaks about AIDS, it does so with real authority. No other organization in Africa is closer to AIDS sufferers. The Church knows the problem firsthand.
- Condoms have proven effective in reducing infection rates among targeted populations of people engaging in high-risk behaviors, such as prostitutes, but not among the population at large. Campaigns pushing condoms send the opposite message to the one that needs to be given.
- Over-reliance on the promotion of condoms misses the heart of the problem. It is time to put more investment into programs aimed at behavior maintenance among the young (many of whom are abstinent and want to remain so until marriage) and behavior change among the young and not-so-young.
- Programs which deal with the underlying problem of promiscuity are the most effective of all. The Church has pioneered behavior-change programs which not only urge chastity and fidelity but help young people resist sexual advances of older relatives and others, known as "sugar daddies" and "sugar mommies." This has helped to reduce transmission rates substantially.
- The Church does urge prostitutes to change their lives for the better and, where possible, helps them to do so. Telling them to use, or not use, condoms is beside the point. Using a condom to prevent infecting another may turn out to be a step in the direction of growing moral responsibility, but that does not justify the promiscuous act.

Chapter 8

KEEP MARRIAGE CONJUGAL

— Challenging Questions —

- *Gay people these days often live in stable, loving relationships, sometimes with children. Why shouldn't they also be allowed to marry?*
- *Gay people are born that way. Surely it is discrimination to exclude them for life from an institution which confers legitimacy and happiness.*
- *Society is stronger when the ties that bind us are stronger. The state should allow gay marriage in order to encourage commitment.*
- *There was strong opposition in the 1950s to interracial marriage, but people came around. It's the same with same-sex marriage. It will come to seem normal over time. Meanwhile, it is sad to see the Catholic Church endorsing prejudice.*

Ten countries in the world and six states in the United States have redefined marriage to include same-sex couples. The first country was the Netherlands (2001), followed two years later by Belgium, countries which pride themselves on permissive legislation on issues such as abortion and euthanasia. They were joined by Canada (2005), which redefined marriage as "the lawful union of two persons to the exclusion of all others." More recently same-sex marriage has been created by Norway, Sweden, and Iceland (2009-10), along with Spain (2005), South Africa (2006), and Portugal and Argentina in 2010 — countries with a history of authoritarian regimes from which modern governments are eager to distance themselves. The United Kingdom and Australia, too, have embarked on the road to what advocates describe as "marriage equality." Other countries are set to follow.

The federal government does not recognize same-sex marriage in the United States, a matter made clear in the 1996 DOMA (Defense of

Marriage Act), which determines that "the word 'marriage' means only a legal union between one man and one woman as husband and wife, and the word 'spouse' refers only to a person of the opposite sex who is a husband or wife." But since Massachusetts became the first state to grant marriage licenses to same-sex couples in 2004, the states of Connecticut, Iowa, New Hampshire, New York, and Vermont have all followed suit. In Pope Benedicts XVI's words, there are "powerful political and cultural currents seeking to alter the legal definition of marriage."

In 2011, it became clear that advocacy of gay marriage is no longer the preserve of liberals and the left. The Conservative British prime minister declared that he is in favor *because* he is a conservative: "Conservatives believe in the ties that bind us; that society is stronger when we make vows to each other and support each other," he told a party meeting. The mayor of New York, Michael Bloomberg, a prominent Republican, argued that supporting same-sex marriage was consistent with conservative principles of limited government and personal liberty. Conservatives, he said, "believe that government should not stand in the way of free markets and private associations, including contracts between consenting parties." He added: "That's exactly what marriage is: a contract, a legal bond, between two adults who vow to support one another, in sickness and in health."

For advocates of "marriage equality," same-sex marriage is the latest stage in the history of the emancipation of homosexual people, a history that began with the lifting of laws criminalizing homosexual acts and moved to the banning of discrimination against gay people in the workplace. In the last twenty years or so, the movement has sought to legitimize gay relationships and put them on a public standing similar to heterosexual ones, in three main areas. First, in many countries gay-rights lobbies have persuaded governments to introduce civil-partnership schemes which confer rights and privileges similar to those enjoyed by married couples, such as inheritance rights, hospital-visiting rights, tax breaks, and so on. Second, they have sought to legalize same-sex adoption, which is now allowed in eight countries around the world and in most U.S. states. Third, they have sought to abolish the commonplace restriction of marriage to a man and a woman, to allow for couples of the same sex to get married.

In the narrative supporting these changes, they are all part of the same struggle for "gay rights." Yet rights cannot be infinitely extended without imposing on other rights — and indeed, the common good of society. It is one thing for the state to protect a minority from prejudice by decriminalizing homosexual acts and criminalizing acts of hatred against homosexual people, something which justice (the equal dignity of gay people) requires. It is quite another for the state to promote same-sex relationships as equal to conjugal marriage. Campaigners for gay marriage will try to elide those two acts, and claim that it is illogical to do the first without the second. In reality, they are of a wholly different logical and legal order.

The Church's objection to "gay marriage" — an artificial term, given the intrinsic meaning of marriage as heterosexual, but we'll use it for the sake of brevity — is precisely to this attempt to overthrow the intrinsic meaning of marriage. That is what legalizing gay marriage involves. By choosing to recognize as "marriage" a union of two people of the same sex, the state has to first reject the definition of marriage as intrinsically conjugal — a union of husband and wife for the primary task of begetting and nurturing children.

Once that definition of marriage is rejected, it is not just gay marriage that becomes possible, but any kind of emotional or sexual partnership such as polygamy or polyamory; and, therefore, marriage ceases to have any plausible meaning at all. Once marriage can mean any combination of committed, sexually involved people, it means nothing. The state has given up on the idea of marriage as an institution that needs to be upheld for the good of children and society.

This is not a theological view. The conjugal definition of marriage has long been upheld, across the ages and by different cultures, as an institution for the purpose of bearing and nurturing children and the good of society. It is a meaning not contingent on any religious definition — although the world's great faiths have recognized and reinforced its meaning, along with every human culture and civilization.

cs

Positive Intention

There are many positive values invoked by advocates of gay marriage. If restricting marriage to a man plus a woman really were discrimination — namely, irrational prejudice against people who don't conform to the social majority — then it would, of course, be wrong; and gay marriage would be a positive move. Equally, if the purpose of marriage were solely to support and encourage commitment between people, then gay marriage would contribute to that end; and certainly there would be no grounds for excluding gay people from marriage. Nor would there be grounds for excluding any relationship where commitment were involved. If the intention behind gay marriage is to encourage such caring, committed relationships, then that is a good intention.

∞

In contrast to Mayor Bloomberg's view of marriage as a private contract, Western society has always upheld marriage as a public social institution recognized and supported by the state because of its benefits to children and society as a whole. It also has an intrinsic meaning, spelled out by religious leaders in a January 2012 letter called "Marriage and Religious Freedom: Fundamental Goods that Stand or Fall Together." The letter begins:

> The promotion and protection of marriage — the union of one man and one woman as husband and wife — is a matter of the common good and serves the well-being of the couple, of children, of civil society, and all people. The meaning and value of marriage precedes and transcends any particular society, government, or religious community. It is a universal good and the foundational institution of all societies. It is bound up with the nature of the human person as male and female, and with the essential task of bearing and nurturing children.

The Church opposes gay marriage, in essence, because it rejects that definition of marriage and replaces it with another definition which renders it non-conjugal. Put positively, Catholics think the state should continue to promote conjugal marriage, not because it wishes to exclude or disapprove or reject any particular group but because:
1. the family is the founding unit of civil society, the vital building block on which human society is built;
2. at the heart of the family is the sexual union of a man and a woman given to each other for their sake and for the good of their children; and

3.   conjugal marriage provides the ideal, irreplaceable environment for the raising of children, who benefit psychologically, emotionally, and in countless other ways from it; and that is why it should be advocated and encouraged by the state.

This is the frame which needs to replace the false narrative that gay-marriage advocates impose on the Church, as if the Church were "supporting discrimination" or "discriminating against gay people." As we saw in Chapter 2, the Church is not an opponent, but a proponent, of the legitimate rights and equality of gay people. Meanwhile, the idea that Catholic opposition to gay marriage is driven by a moral repudiation of homosexual acts is simply false; the Church has strongly and consistently backed measures to end the criminalization and marginalization of gay people, and to allow them to play a full part in society. Just as people should not be negatively defined by their faith, creed, or gender, nor should they be defined by their sexual orientation: people are first of all *people*, human beings created in the image of God, and they have an intrinsic right to be respected as such, whatever their orientation or actions.

But the Church does not accept that this principle can be invoked to justify the state redefining marriage in such a way as to make the union of a man and a woman and the generation of offspring irrelevant to it. The Church is not "against the right of gay people to marriage" so much as "in favor of keeping conjugal marriage special." That is not to advocate "discrimination." It is no more discriminatory to restrict marriage to a man and a woman than it is to restrict Social Security entitlements to those who have reached a certain age.

Catholics opposing same-sex marriage are sometimes likened to racists who objected to interracial marriage in some American states in the past. This is a major category error. Precisely *because* marriage is between a man and a woman — any man and any woman who as single adults may freely and consciously choose it — any attempt to restrict marriage on the basis of race or class goes against the nature of marriage itself. To exclude anyone on racial or social grounds is eugenicist. To attempt to align the Church to such ideas, which it has always vociferously condemned, is offensive and misguided. It is in the nature of marriage for men and women to cross boundaries of race, class, and nation in order to be together for life, just as it is in the nature of marriage for there to be a man and a woman, brought together in biological union.

Every law makes distinctions. There is nothing unjustly discriminatory in relying on genuinely relevant distinctions. Equality is not equivalence. States and churches have always imposed restrictions on marriage, where these are reasonable, in order to support the nature and meaning of the institution. Gay people "born that way" are unable to marry; so, too, are direct relatives, or people with psychological or physical impediments. People entering marriage need to be capable of understanding its obligations and assuming them, which excludes those underage or not of sound mind. They must enter marriage of their own volition, which excludes those who are being coerced against their will. They must be two individuals, rather than multiple partners; and they must be a man and a woman. This excludes bigamous and same-sex, as well as open, temporary, polyamorous and polyandrous unions.

If it is discriminatory to exclude same-sex unions, then it must also be discriminatory to exclude these others. The only way of abolishing all "discrimination" in marriage is for the state to cease recognizing marriages in law, and make it an entirely private matter, as Mayor Bloomberg seems to think it already is. But if the state is to continue to recognize marriage, it must continue to define it and set boundaries on it.

Those boundaries have been designed to protect essential features such as monogamy and sexual complementarity, which can be summarized in the word "conjugal." If the state renounces conjugality as an essential feature of marriage, there can be no basis for excluding relatives or bigamists, and this will open the path to claims for these, too, to be allowed to marry. This isn't simply a "slippery slope" rhetorical scare tactic; some slopes really do slip. In Canada in 2011 a group of fundamentalist Mormons argued that, since the British Columbia Supreme Court had changed the definition of marriage to allow for same-sex marriage in such a way that it no longer was defined as *one man and one woman* in a monogamous relationship, it should now be changed to allow for *men and women* in a polygamous relationship. The Court ruled against the Mormons, arguing that monogamous marriage had been "a fundamental value in Western society from the earliest of times." Yet in 2003, when the Court ruled in favor of gay marriage, it did not consider sexual complementarity in marriage "a fundamental value in Western society from the earliest times."

Restricting marriage to a man and a woman in a monogamous union is reasonable, not discriminatory, because such restrictions support the intrinsically conjugal meaning of marriage. That is why there is no "right to same-sex marriage" in international charters such as the European Convention on Human Rights (ECHR).

The reframing of this issue, therefore, must move the question away from the "equality-rights" frame and toward another which answers the question of what marriage is, what it is for, and why it has been legally enshrined. This is not an issue about gay rights versus any other rights, but about the meaning and purpose of marriage, and why the state should single it out and promote it. And it is about what happens when the state changes its meaning and purpose, renouncing its preference for conjugal marriage: it is about the long-term consequences for children and society in general. Once these are grasped, it will be clear why gay people, whether people of faith or not, are among the strongest critics of same-sex "marriage."

A Common-Good Case

There are many reasons why Christians back marriage. Catholics regard it as a sacrament, an instrument of God's grace and of sanctification of those involved. For evangelicals, marriage is rooted in the first chapters of Genesis.

But it is not a good idea to start the case for marriage here. Those arguments are heard as one group in society seeking to impose its views on others. The state has no obligation to agree with, even less demand adherence to, the presuppositions of one faith or indeed any faith. And because changing the law to allow same-sex marriage involves reforming *civil* marriage — the definition of marriage upheld by the state — an appeal to theological presuppositions invites the accusation of religious interference in the secular.

It is also a category error. We should not appeal to religious arguments when objecting to changes to an institution which is not intrinsically religious or subject to religious control. Marriage as an institution long predates Christianity, and is present in every culture, whatever its faith.

That said, the introduction of same-sex marriage will have many consequences for religious freedom. As the religious leaders noted in their

January 2012 letter, the fear is not that priests and ministers will be forced to conduct same-sex weddings in religious institutions; the First Amendment would preclude that. It is rather that the law would come to treat same-sex sexual conduct as the moral equivalent of marital sexual conduct, leading to religious organizations facing civil liability suits as well as the withdrawal of government grants and benefits. The letter noted:

> By a single stroke, every law where rights depend on marital status — such as employment discrimination, employment benefits, adoption, education, health care, elder care, housing, property, and taxation — will change so that same-sex sexual relationships must be treated as if they were marriage. That requirement, in turn, will apply to religious people and groups in the ordinary course of their many private or public occupations and ministries — including running schools, hospitals, nursing homes and other housing facilities, providing adoption and counseling services, and many others.

These are very real fears. But the threat to religious freedom cannot be the substance of any objection to same-sex "marriage." The focus must be instead on the common-good case against it, and the implications for society — and especially for children — of changing the law.

Indeed, the point about marriage is that it is an institution which belongs to neither Church nor state. It is a natural institution, one deeply embedded in civil society, which is regulated by the state but not created by it, any more than it has been created by the Church. Most people would acknowledge that marriage involves a union of a man and a woman, a special link to children, and norms of permanence, monogamy, and exclusivity. A "real" marriage is one that conforms to this conjugal character.

Marriage is not merely a social and legal construct; its existence is recognized by the law of both state and Church, but these do not "create" the marriage. And that is why the state's attempt to change its meaning involves the state going beyond its competence: It involves, as author George Weigel has pointed out, "a vast expansion of state power." The state, seeking to satisfy the demands of an interest group seeking legitimacy through legal recognition, is reaching deep into civil society in an attempt to alter its architecture.

In a paper for the Catholic Education Resource Center, Katharine Young and Paul Nathanson have discovered that marriage across cultures and historical periods contains a number of universal features as well as nearly universal ones. Its universal features include the fact that marriage is supported by authority and incentives; rests on the interdependence of men and women; has a public, or communal, dimension; defines eligible partners; encourages procreation; and provides mutual support not only between men and women, but also between them and children. Its nearly universal features are: an emphasis on durable relationships between parents; mutual affection and companionship; and reciprocity between young and old. Underlying all these features, however, Young and Nathanson identify one vital overriding purpose of marriage — that it encourages heterosexual bonding, bringing men and women together for life for children. That purpose, they conclude, is of overriding importance to all human societies in all places and at all times.

In summary, marriage exists and is promoted for three essential reasons: to encourage the birth and upbringing of children, to provide the best possible setting for children to grow up in, and to ensure the cooperation of men and women for the common good.

Those reasons tell us about the intrinsic nature of marriage. Living together in a committed relationship is not a sufficient criterion. Nor is being sexually involved. Rearing children together is not enough to make a marriage. Equally, same-sex partnerships, whatever their moral status, cannot be marriages because they lack an essential orientation to children; even when a sexual act is involved, it cannot be generative.

Although religion has taken these elements and deepened their meaning in the light of revelation, a person does not need to be religious to grasp their importance. That is why the Catholic argument against gay marriage is not, essentially, religious, but is made from reason and natural law. Marriage is a public social institution, singled out and promoted by state, faith, and civil society, because it serves a far-reaching social good. Every child who has ever been born has been created by a mother and a father; and every society has always regarded this fact as of such significance that marriage — the institution which brings together a man and a woman to provide a place of nurture for that child — has been elevated to the status of a social institution.

In other words, at the heart of what makes marriage special and deserving of promotion by the state is precisely its conjugal nature. As the

Catholic bishops of New York said in 2009: "The state has a compelling legal interest in promoting marriage between men and women in order to create stable families and provide for the safety, health and well-being of children. The state has no such compelling legal interest in recognizing a relationship between two people of the same sex." If there are injustices against those in relationships other than marriage, they added, "those injustices can certainly be reformed and corrected in other ways."

This can be put another way: If marriage is no longer defined as conjugal, the state no longer has a reason to promote it. The reason for promoting it — to encourage the biological union of man and woman, which gives rise to the best possible environment for children — has disappeared. What happens, then, to the children?

An Institution Geared to Children

A conjugal relationship is much more than a sexual relationship; it is a sexual relationship which, by its nature, produces children. Even when a married couple cannot have children, they are still capable of offering a child a home with a mother and a father. The fact that a particular couple cannot have children — because they are too old or infertile — does not alter the fact that men and women are by nature capable of doing so. When the law restricts marriage to a man plus a woman, it is recognizing that fact.

By upholding conjugal marriage, the law recognizes that children raised by their biological parents are in a uniquely beneficial position. Children fare best when they are raised by their biological parents in a low-conflict marriage. It is in their interest, and in the interest of society as a whole, that as many children as possible are raised by their biological parents — as long as they are not abusive or neglectful. That is why the government's social policy should be to encourage this outcome by all possible means.

Of course, marriage does not exist solely for children; and people do not marry solely for the purpose of having children. There are many social goods which marriage encourages — commitment, fidelity, and stability, for example. But the reason the state promotes marriage is because marriage is best for children. As endless studies demonstrate, children in low-conflict married homes are less likely to suffer child poverty, sexual and physical abuse, or mental or physical ill health; they are less likely to misuse drugs, commit crimes, suffer disadvantage in the workplace, or become divorced and unwed parents themselves. The weight of social-science evidence strongly supports the idea that family structure matters and that children do best when raised by their own mother and father in a decent, loving marriage. It is not simply the presence of two parents, but the presence of two *biological* parents, that best supports children's development. That's why the state promotes marriage by singling it out in law.

There are two common objections raised to this argument. The first is that, while the ideal is unarguable, the reality is that marriage has, in fact, broken down to the point where there are at least as many children born out of wedlock as within it; for the state to promote marriage is like trying to close the barn door after the horse has run off. The answer to this is well expressed by Ron Haskins and Isabel Sawhill in a 2004 Brookings Institute book, *Creating an Opportunity Society*, which recommends pro-marriage policies as one key way to help the poor. "Marriage brings not only clear economic benefits but social benefits as well, enabling children to grow up to be more successful than they might otherwise be," they point out. "To those who argue that this goal [of promoting marriage] is old-fashioned or inconsistent with modern culture, we argue that modern culture is inconsistent with the needs of children."

The second common objection comes from some proponents of gay marriage, who point out that children raised by same-sex couples fare just as well as those raised by a mother and father, and cite studies to this effect. Almost all of these studies are of lesbian, rather than gay couples, bringing up children. They are extremely limited in scope, based on self-selecting samples, are not longitudinal — that is, do not track the welfare of children over time — and often ask the couple concerned to comment on their view of how the child is faring. The fact is that same-sex adoption has simply not been around or been practiced long enough for anyone to claim a "scientific" basis for the assertion that children fare as well. The same claim could be made just as easily for the children of single or divorced parents.

And it would be beside the point. When the state promotes (conjugal) marriage as uniquely beneficial for children, it is not declaring official disapproval of the myriad other ways children are being brought up. It condemns no one. Millions of children are brought up in less than ideal circumstances — by single parents, divorced parents, stepparents, aunts and uncles, same-sex couples — and often benefit from great love and care. Sometimes these arrangements are saving children from a much worse fate; it might be better for a child to be brought up by a same-sex couple than to remain, for example, in an orphanage. But at the same time, it would be foolish to deny that in all these cases children are deprived of something they need for a healthy psychological upbringing. The law upholds what is in the *best* interest of children. What is in their best interest is not a same-sex couple, or a single parent, or divorced parents — however loving these may be.

In the case of a single parent, the child yearns for the missing mother or father. In the case of a same-sex couple, children are deprived of the chance to relate equally well to the other sex. It is not the sexual *orientation* of the people bringing up a child which is relevant to that child's well-being, but their sexual *complementarity*. As the openly gay *Spectator* columnist Matthew Parris acknowledges: "I'm glad I had both a mother and father, and that after childhood I was to spend my life among both men and women, and as men and women are not the same, I would have missed something if I had not learned first about the world from, and with, both a woman and a man, and in the love of both."

Marriage has traditionally been recognized as coming into being when consummation occurs. The laws of both Church and state have traditionally recognized non-consummation as grounds for dissolving the marriage. The bodily union integral to marriage is rooted in its link to procreation. Hence the norms which traditionally surround marriage designed to foster stable and harmonious conditions which are undermined by divorce and infidelity: these are all geared to children. In relationships which lack this orientation to children, it is hard to see why permanence and exclusivity should be normative, and even harder to understand why the state should promote them.

What It Means to Abandon the Meaning of Marriage

Given that the number who choose a gay marriage is likely to be very small — in Spain, for example, only two thousand same-sex couples have chosen to "marry" since the law was introduced in 2005 — how would this "small concession" to a minority change things for the majority?

The answer is that it would weaken marriage, obscure the value of opposite-sex parenting, and undermine moral and religious freedom.

Society takes its cue from cultural norms, which are partly reflected in, and partly shaped by, the law. In redefining marriage, the state would now teach that marriage is concerned with emotional unions — that is, friendship — rather than biological union or children. Because there is no reason why friendship should be permanent, exclusive, or limited to two, the norms of marriage of permanence, exclusivity, and monogamy would make little sense. In their paper in the *Harvard Journal of Law & Public Policy* titled "What Is Marriage?", authors Sherif Girgis, Robert P. George, and Ryan T. Anderson note: "Less able to understand the rationale for these marital norms, people would feel less bound to live by them. And less able to understand the value of marriage itself as a certain kind of union . . . people would increasingly fail to see the intrinsic reasons they have for marrying or staying with a spouse absent consistently strong feeling."

Too late, some might say: developments over the last fifty years in Western culture have chipped away at the norms of marriage, and society no longer knows what it means. Yet recent surveys find that just over half of the adult U.S. population is married. The institution may be crying out for stronger cultural encouragement, but it is very far from defunct. The idea that same-sex marriage would provide such encouragement, as the British prime minister seems to think, is severely misplaced. Although it is impossible to prove a causal link, the divorce rate in Spain has soared since 2005, when same-sex marriage was legalized there. A year later, it was announced that Spanish birth certificates would read "Progenitor A" and "Progenitor B" instead of "father" and "mother."

It makes sense. By overthrowing the notion of a husband and wife as the most appropriate environment for children, fewer children would be brought up by their parents, and the state would need to play an even larger role in their health, education, and welfare. Of necessity, it would become the official policy of the state and public institutions that it does not matter whether a child is the offspring of a biological union of mother and father or whether he or she is brought up by a same-sex couple. The result of this would be, logically, that no kind of arrangement for bringing up children could any longer be proposed as an ideal, and to suggest otherwise would be "discriminatory."

Introducing gay marriage is not an example of value-neutrality; as the political philosopher Michael Sandel notes in his book *Justice*, "the case for same-sex marriage can't be made on nonjudgmental grounds. It depends on a certain conception of the *telos* of marriage — its purpose or point." The debate about the purpose of a social institution is a debate about the virtues it honors and rewards; "the underlying moral question," Sandel says, "is unavoidable."

If the state were to cease to give legal recognition to marriage of any kind, leaving it to private associations, the question would not arise. But no modern state has done so. Because governments wish to encourage marriage, they must necessarily define its purpose and nature. In introducing same-sex marriage, governments have to redefine the purpose of marriage as being not about the begetting and rearing of children, but about merely the commitment of two people to each other. As Pope Benedict says, "Sexual differences cannot be dismissed as irrelevant to the definition of marriage."

That would be the state's position, to be accepted by all public employees. By redefining marriage in this way, the state must necessarily come to a view that the supporters of conjugal marriage are bigots and must be treated like racists. Anti-discrimination legislation in this way has become a mechanism for dethroning marriage as a state privileged by law, and for enthroning a new principle — that same-sex unions are equivalent to marriage between a man and a woman, and same-sex adoption is equivalent to adoption by a mother and father. Thereafter it is a small step to compel all institutions to accept that principle or face the consequences (as has occurred with Catholic adoption agencies, as we saw in Chapter 3). Thus, says Pope Benedict XVI in *Light of the World*, "in the name of tolerance, tolerance is being abolished."

଼

EXISTING FRAME

"Gay marriage is simply the latest chapter in the emancipation of gay people. Allowing gay people to marry is an issue of basic gay equality, and those who oppose their right to do so are in favor of discrimination. Many of them are religious; they want their holy books

to dictate laws, imposing their view of sexuality on the rest of society. They must be resisted, and after a time they will come round, just as did all those people back in the 1950s who said you couldn't have people of two different races getting married. The fact is gay people enter into committed, loving relationships for life, and many of them bring up children in loving, stable homes. Why shouldn't they be given the chance for the legitimacy and social approval that marriage brings? Why should they be second-class citizens?"

REFRAME

This is a question about what marriage means and whether the state should support that meaning. Marriage has always and everywhere been understood as a lifelong union between a man and a woman for the sake of their offspring. The state has upheld that meaning and promoted it because of its unique and irreplaceable benefits for children and for society as a whole. If the state now redefines marriage so that it is no longer about a man and a woman, then the state is no longer promoting marriage. This isn't about gay rights. It's about the right of children to have the state protect their best interests — and study after study shows that their best interests lie in being brought up by their biological parents bound to each other for life. If the state creates "gay marriage," it is saying the best interests of children — and society as a whole — no longer matter. The implications of that are very serious indeed. The Church does not seek to impose a theological view of marriage; it respects civil marriage. But it cannot be silent when the interests of children and the common good of society are discarded under the false pretext of ending discrimination.

 প্র

Key Messages

- This is not an issue about equality. To give everyone equal access to marriage would require the state to cease to recognize marriage altogether. This debate is about the purpose of marriage and why the state should promote it.
- The state cannot be neutral. It has to promote an idea of marriage. Either it is conjugal or it is not. If it is not conjugal, there is no reason for the state to promote one set of relationships over another.

- The demand for gay marriage is not a demand for marriage to be extended to gay people; it is a demand for marriage to be redefined. The idea of marriage as a biological union of a man and a woman for children will be redefined as being for an emotional commitment between two people. Children will be irrelevant. That has consequences for children.
- Once gay marriage is allowed, there are no reasonable grounds for refusing to admit other forms of relationship. Once marriage means any kind of committed, sexual relationship, it means nothing at all.
- Allowing gay marriage would undermine marriage, be bad for children, and curb religious freedom.
- Marriage belongs to neither state nor Church, but is a natural institution which both should recognize. By trying to redefine it, the state is overreaching.

Chapter 9

WOMEN AND THE CHURCH

— Challenging Questions —

- *Why does the Church think women aren't good enough to be priests?*
- *Why, when Jesus opened up new opportunities for women, has the Church sought to deny them a public role?*
- *If the Church opposes the two great achievements of women's emancipation — contraception and abortion — how can it be in favor of women?*
- *Why are there so few women working in the Vatican?*

The twentieth-century women's movement has challenged both society and the Church to face up to their exclusion of the female voice and presence. The anger of feminism is the product of genuine grievances. As Pope John Paul II said in his 1995 *Letter to Women*, history has placed many obstacles in women's path to progress. "Women's dignity has often been unacknowledged and their prerogatives misrepresented; they have often been relegated to the margins of society and even reduced to servitude," he wrote. "This has prevented women from truly being themselves, and it has resulted in a spiritual impoverishment of humanity."

And for this he apologized on behalf of the Church: "If objective blame, especially in particular historical contexts, has belonged to not just a few members of the Church, for this I am truly sorry."

But if the record of the Church, no less than society, is marked by failure on this point, it is important to understand how deeply embedded patriarchalism has been in all societies, long before Christianity appeared. The notion that a woman, like children, is the property of a man without distinct social and legal personality was broadly shared in all ancient societies. What is remarkable is how this assumption was challenged by Christianity, building on the Old Testament empathy with the outsider and victim.

Few can question the importance of women in the Church's life and devotions: the honor given to Jesus' mother, Mary, *Theotokos* ("God-bearer"), and the myriad saints from the virgin martyrs of the first centuries of Christianity up to Mother Teresa of Calcutta, not to mention the great women doctors of the Church (Catherine of Siena, Teresa of Avila, Thérèse of Lisieux, and Hildegard of Bingen). All these testify to the presence of the feminine, which Catholicism has integrated rather better than other faiths or denominations. The great Swiss psychoanalyst Carl Jung praised the proclamation by Pius XII of the dogma of the Assumption in 1950 as the most important religious event for 400 years. Together with the dogma of the Immaculate Conception a century earlier, he believed that it re-established the feminine element in human understanding of God's nature, which he saw as having been rejected or downplayed in post-Reformation Christianity, especially Protestantism.

But the question of the Church and women is not just about the presence of the feminine in prayer and piety, but the place of women in the public life of the Church — and of Catholic women in wider society. In an era when the feminist movement has sought to overturn the legal, cultural, and political exclusion of women, a narrative has been created in which the Church is the enemy of that emancipation. Yet the Church, as we shall see, is one of the great advocates in the modern world of overcoming patriarchalism and liberating what Pope John Paul II, in *Mulieris Dignitatem*, calls the "feminine genius."

The "new" feminism advocated by that apostolic letter on the dignity and vocation of women seeks to purify feminism from its attachment to perverted masculine values. Rather than rejecting biological differences between men and women, it sees those differences as essential; rather than rejecting women as mothers, it sees their capacity for motherhood as endowing women with particular, exceptional gifts and abilities, both practical and spiritual, which are key to the salvation of the world — not least in public life.

ભ

POSITIVE INTENTION

Behind criticism of the Church as the upholder of patriarchy conceals a very Christian assumption that men and women are of equal value and dignity. It follows that where the Church has failed to hear the

*voice of women or has excluded them, and where that exclusion has
been supported by Catholic doctrines and theologies, the Church must
acknowledge fault. There is also a positive intention behind the criticism of stereotyping: women are called into a huge variety of roles. The
positive intention behind the women's movement becomes less positive,
however, when it pushes equality (of worth and dignity) to the point
where it seeks to emulate what are essentially perverted male values of
power and domination. Female emancipation will only be authentic
when it is able to subvert, and not merely emulate, structures currently
dominated by (often perverted) male values.*

∝

Women and the Early Church

The Gospel opened new horizons for women. Luke's account of the
Incarnation shows the equal worth and dignity of women in God's eyes
by his choosing women characters to mirror men. And he reversed their
social roles: although women at the time were considered property with
no legal rights, and men spoke on their behalf, in Luke's narrative the
men remain silent, are struck dumb, or ask to be dismissed in peace,
while the women rejoice as God acts, speaking out and prophesying.

The women of the Gospels, and above all Mary, recall many of the
women hidden in the Old Testament who left their mark on history, in
spite of the best efforts of a male-dominated narrative. There is Miriam,
who had equal status as a leader with Moses and Aaron in the exodus
from Egypt, who sings the song of liberation (see Ex 15:21) later echoed
by Mary; or Deborah, one of the divinely chosen leaders or Judges who
led an army against Israel's enemy (Jgs 4) — just as, later, St. Joan of Arc
would lead troops into battle in fifteenth-century France.

It is a matter of record that Jesus was extraordinarily responsive to,
respectful of, and indebted to women, and he counted them among
his prominent disciples and dearest associates. Luke mentions Mary of
Magdala, Joanna, Susanna and "many others" (see Lk 8:2-3). Then there
are various women with different roles of responsibility around Jesus,
who, unlike the Twelve Apostles, did not abandon Jesus in the hour of his
passion. Among them, Mary Magdalene stands out in particular — the
first witness and herald of the Resurrection.

It is also a matter of record that Christianity was attractive to women, and changed the way they were treated: the Christian sexual ethic, for example, differed from pagan standards in regarding a husband's unfaithfulness as no less serious a breach than a wife's. And at a time when divorce was a male privilege — by the law of Moses a woman could not divorce her husband — Jesus' insistence on marriage as a lifelong bond was a strongly pro-woman teaching. "Going beyond the social and religious barriers of the time, Jesus re-established woman in her full dignity as a human person before God and before men," Pope John Paul II said in 1979. "Christ's way of acting, the Gospel of his words and deeds, is a consistent protest against whatever offends the dignity of women."

Saint Paul's doctrine that in Christ is neither male nor female, free man or slave (see Gal 3:28) did not question the social role of women any more than it actively sought to end slavery; but by elevating their status by insisting that they are created in God's image and redeemed in Christ, and must therefore be treated with sovereign respect, he laid the foundation of their later emancipation. The modern movements for women's rights are the outworking of this principle.

In the early Church women took on vital, varied roles: teaching, preaching, prophesying, preparing for baptism, hosting church functions. In the Acts of the Apostles, the stories of Lydia, the first baptized convert in Europe — like Tabitha, a single woman — shows how in a short time the social roles had changed: the fact that women could constitute an embryonic Church but not the synagogue reveals difference in status between the two faiths. Where the Gospel spread, women were among the first and foremost disciples and played crucial roles in developing the early Church. Across the first-century Mediterranean world we find women being converted and serving the community in roles that would normally have been available to them only apart from the community.

Yet at the same time as he affirmed and strengthened the roles of women, Jesus chose twelve men as apostles. Respect for this choice, seen as highly significant by the Catholic and Orthodox Churches, is the reason for their continuing to reserve the priesthood to men. Yet to do so is not a rejection or refusal of the gifts and equal dignity of women, but a means by which God converts male authority into service while promoting the unique but different power of women.

What confuses this issue is clericalism. Clericalism is a view of religious leaders as a superior social caste, which Jesus put a great deal of effort into rejecting; much of what he tells and shows the Twelve is one long argument against such attitudes. Yet despite the new possibilities for women opened by Christianity, historians show how within a short time — within two or three hundred years of Jesus' death and resurrection — that progress slowed, under pressure from persecution. Concerned that Christians did not attract attention for the wrong reasons, it is not surprising that Paul should be exhorting wives to obey husbands, slaves to obey their masters, and everyone to obey the governing authorities.

Opportunities for women also slowed when Christianity became the official religion of the Roman Empire in the fourth century, and at the same time more socially conformist. Yet women remained prominent in the life of the early Church, dying heroic deaths in Rome's Colosseum rather than deny their faith in Christ, and being honored from the earliest days as being, like Mary, the greatest followers of Christ. As mystics, missionaries, martyrs, and founders of new orders and communities, women were crucial to the growth of Christianity.

This was particularly true in the seventh, eighth, and ninth centuries, when the expansion of the Church in Europe was led by the monasteries. There were more than thirty abbesses in Britain alone — among them St. Hilda of Whitby and St. Etheldreda of Ely — acclaimed as saints by the early Church. They presided over often vast agricultural regions, established centers of learning, convened synods, and led and guided huge communities of both men and women.

The point about these great women is not just that they were holy and inspiring, but that they were *leaders* in the modern sense of the term. Abbesses such as Hildegard of Bingen were consulted by bishops and popes, exercised very real authority, and had a huge influence, both through the offices they held and their gifts of teaching and preaching, over not just their own communities but the wider Church. If a male priesthood or the doctrines of Christianity led to the subordination and exclusion of women, it would be impossible for this to happen. Yet great offices were held by women in the Church, just as they are today. (The Focolare movement, established in northern Italy after World War II, and now numbering hundreds of thousands worldwide, has both men and women members, but by its own statutes must be led by a woman.)

This is not to claim that women in the Church's history have been equal, or to deny that they have been excluded; it is to claim that, in spite of the obstacles of widespread patriarchy and misogyny in wider society, in the Church there could be great public women, and that a male priesthood was not in itself an obstacle to their assuming such roles. The all-female religious communities of the Middle Ages offered opportunities for education and influence that were denied all but the most aristocratic women of the time.

Of course, they frequently battled with authorities who refused to allow women to speak and act for themselves. The story of Mary Ward may be typical. When she created an order of apostolic sisters in England in 1609 it quickly caught on, and within twenty years there were schools and communities across Europe educating women to do great things. But Church authorities, in keeping with the mores of the time, were scandalized by women claiming their public space, and the Institute of the Blessed Virgin Mary (now the Congregation of Jesus) was suppressed, and Ward herself imprisoned by the Inquisition as a heretic. Three hundred years later, in 1909, long after orders of apostolic sisters were the norm in the Church, Mary Ward and her work were fully vindicated. The Church has often taken time to translate principles into practice.

Women in the Church Today: A Journey Unfinished

The twentieth-century social, economic, cultural, and political emancipation of women was recognized in the strongest terms in the closing message of the Second Vatican Council. "The hour is coming, in fact has come, when the vocation of women is being acknowledged in its fullness, the hour in which women acquire in the world an influence, an effect and a power never hitherto achieved," the message read, adding a call for women to take their place.

That meant in the Church's structures too, as Pope Paul VI made clear in 1970. "It is evident that women are meant to form part of the living and working structure of Christianity," he acknowledged, after declaring Saint Catherine of Siena and Saint Teresa of Avila Doctors of the Church, adding that "not all their potentialities have yet been made clear." Since then women have come to play a much fuller role in the leadership of church organizations. This is especially true in Western countries, where social expectations about women's roles have most changed, and where women have long had access to education and other forms of social capital.

In the Vatican, too, there has been progress, even if it has been gla-
cial. There were no women at all working in the Roman Curia before
1952, but by the end of John Paul II's pontificate in 2005, according to
a Catholic News Service report, women made up 21 percent of Vatican
personnel.

Very few, though, have made it to decision-making levels. At a
meeting with the clergy of Rome in 2006, Pope Benedict XVI said it
was right "to ask whether in ministerial service . . . it might be possible
to make more room, to give more offices of responsibility to women."
Yet five years after those remarks, there are only two women in decision-
making roles, both serving as undersecretaries; and only one agency in
the Vatican — the Academy for Social Sciences — headed by a woman,
American law professor Mary Ann Glendon. (There is no female theologian among those advising the Congregation for the Doctrine of
the Faith, for example, and no woman on the commission responsible
for matrimonial cases. On the International Theological Commission,
which advises the congregation on doctrinal issues, there are two wom-
en among the twenty-nine members. And two women serve as consult-
ants to the Council for Promoting the New Evangelization.)

But it is easy to conflate the issue of *women* and Church leadership
with the wider issue of the *laity* and Church leadership. Those roles
which involve not just power of governance but also sacramental power,
continue, naturally, to be occupied by priests. In other words, what can
look like male dominance is in reality clerical dominance. This is especially true in the Vatican, where positions of responsibility have been
traditionally occupied by priests, even in roles for which sacramental
power is not a prerequisite; which is why there are almost as few laymen
in decision-making roles as laywomen. The Vatican, in this sense, is very
much a "clerical club."

But in Church structures which almost every Catholic belongs to
and experiences directly — dioceses, parishes, charitable groups, and
schools — the situation is reversed. Here, women are moving into ministerial roles within the Church "at rates which often surpass those of
comparable institutions in the secular world," according to John Allen's
2009 book *The Future Church*. Looking at current trends he predicts:
"In the trenches, the sociological reality is likely to be that the bulk of
pastoral care offered by Catholic parishes, hospitals, schools, and other
institutions will be delivered by women. Aside from the priesthood and

the episcopacy, ministry in the Catholic Church will progressively become 'women's work.'"

Vatican figures show that the total of clergy and laity involved in the Church's apostolate went from 1.6 million in 1978 to 4.3 million in 2005, about 90 percent of whom were laypeople. This means that nowadays the number of laypeople occupying ministerial positions in the Catholic Church worldwide exceeds the number of clergy by a larger and ever increasing margin. The vast majority of these ministerial posts — teacher, catechist, pastoral assistant — are occupied by women. In the United States in 2007, about 80 percent of 31,000 lay ecclesial ministers — laypeople exercising qualified, recognized ministerial roles — were women, which is why lay ecclesial ministry in the Catholic Church figures in the U.S. Census Bureau data as a job category disproportionately is occupied by women, along with nurses, cashiers, and travel agents. Outside lay ecclesial ministry the proportion of women is lower but still very high: in diocesan administration, for example, just under 50 percent of all positions, and just under a third of all executive positions, are held by women.

These figures hold up very favorably against comparable institutions and are far better than, for example, the business sector. In October 2011, the not-for-profit group Catalyst found that women held just 14 percent of senior executive positions at Fortune 500 companies. The number has barely increased since 2005.

Compared with secular institutions, therefore, the Church has been more open to women. But, of course, most Catholic women do not work or volunteer in the Church, but in the world. Catholic women are to be found at the highest levels of public life, as lawyers, politicians, journalists, teachers, and so on. Far from being inhibited by their faith from assuming those roles, many cite their faith as the specific reason for wanting to be engaged in making the world a better place.

Why Catholic Priests Are Men

Because a male priesthood is not a matter of discipline but a core doctrine of the Church, the question of admitting women to the Catholic priesthood is academic. Various popes have made clear that the choice of men as priests belongs to the deposit of faith, which it is the Church's mission to uphold. There is no power or mechanism by which it could admit women to the priesthood; the Church is "powerless" to do so. Pope John Paul II said in 1994 that "the Church has no authority whatsoever to confer priestly ordination on women" and noted that this was "to be definitively held by all the Church's faithful." Popes do not make such declarations unless they are sure they will not be contradicted in the future.

Because so many other Christian traditions — among them Lutherans, Episcopalians, Methodists, and Baptists — have women clergy, the Catholic and Orthodox Churches look out of step. Consider each Church's view of the Eucharist and priesthood, however, and the divergence is not so surprising. The Catholic and Orthodox conception of the priesthood is very strongly Eucharistic and sacramental. Both Churches believe that an ontological shift takes place at the altar, and that a priest acts *in persona Christi*. The reference point, therefore, is Christ himself; and his maleness is not incidental.

The *Catechism* points out, with plentiful scriptural references: "The Lord Jesus chose men (*viri*) to form the college of the twelve apostles, and the apostles did the same when they chose collaborators to succeed them in their ministry. The college of bishops, with whom the priests are united in the priesthood, makes the college of the twelve an ever-present and ever-active reality until Christ's return. The Church recognizes herself to be bound by this choice made by the Lord himself. For this reason the ordination of women is not possible" (no. 1577).

This is the simplest point of all to be made. The Church regards itself as bound by Jesus' choice of men as apostles, a choice seen as deliberate, significant, and applicable to every age and culture where the Church is present. Why Jesus made that choice, and what it means — both for men and women — calls for deeper reflection.

It is easy to object that history has moved on, and that an all-male priesthood is simply clinging to the past. But that is to misread history. Even in Jesus' time, the "priestess" was an established part of the surrounding religious milieu. So if Jesus chose only men apostles, he was not bowing to the conventions of his age, but defying them — as he did when these were obstacles to his mission. His choice of men as priests has always been considered, therefore, deeply significant. It is why Christians in the early Church always took for granted the idea of the male priesthood, and why the teaching has been clear and consistent in every generation.

Reserving the priesthood to men is not a judgment on women's abilities or rights, any more than celibacy is a judgment on marriage, or marriage a judgment on single people. The teaching reflects the specific role of the priest in the Catholic understanding, which is to represent Jesus, to stand in his place.

As John Paul II wrote in his *Letter to Women*: "These role distinctions should not be viewed in accordance with the criteria of functionality typical in human societies. Rather they must be understood according to the particular criteria of the sacramental economy, i.e., the economy of 'signs' which God freely chooses in order to become present in the midst of humanity."

What "sign" does a male priesthood give? The priesthood is not a career or a job, but a calling, a vocation, and a state of life. And while priests do exercise power — both the power to celebrate sacraments and the power of governance — they are called to do so in a way very different from a patriarchal model. It is possible to speculate, therefore, that one reason why Jesus called men to be priests is that he sought to create a model of male authority that involved service, self-emptying, vulnerability, and openheartedness.

And in so doing, Jesus opened up another kind of power for women. A woman, as much as a man, and in ways that men cannot, can witness to the love of Christ and bring others to him through her example and ministry. All Christians are part of the common priesthood. All are called to holiness. Being a priest or bishop does not make a person more holy. But the Church holds that only a man can represent Jesus in his humanity, a humanity that is not sexually neutral.

Most Catholic women are untroubled by this understanding of the male priesthood, and do not see it as a constraint on their own potential. When Pope John Paul II chose new patron saints for Europe — rulers, prophets, and academics — half were women who had a profound impact on the era they lived in. Saint Bridget of Sweden was a formidable mystic and leader; Saint Catherine of Siena publicly admonished the pope; Saint Edith Stein was a leading German philosopher of the early twentieth century. The Church is not afraid of the abilities of women; it was the Church which first set up schools in Europe to educate them. And looking at the Church across the globe, it is hard not to conclude that women drive the great Catholic enterprises which witness to Christ's love for humanity. And they do not need the priesthood to do it.

A New Feminism

In his 1988 apostolic letter *Mulieris Dignitatem* Pope John Paul II rejected outdated cultural views that God meant women to be subject to men. Both were created in God's image and likeness with equal dignity, he said, noting that "the situations in which the woman remains disadvantaged or discriminated against by the fact of being a woman" are the continuing consequences of sin.

The Church has seen the women's liberation movement as positive insofar as it represents the coming-of-age of an essentially Christian impulse — the equal worth and dignity of women. While defending women's rights, however, Pope John Paul highlighted how women are different from men. Women and men have complementary natures, he taught, and their "diversity of roles" in the Church and in the family reflects that reality.

This idea of an "integral complementarity" between the sexes is a basic tenet of the new feminism pioneered by Catholics responding to Pope John Paul's call. "Discrimination is an evil," says Katrina Zeno in *Every Woman's Journey,* "but distinction is God's design." Men and women are different, and this difference affects the way they live their lives, what they care about, and their strengths and weaknesses. But those differences should never be used to unilaterally discriminate except in cases where a task is subjectively contingent upon a person being of a certain sex (which for Catholic and Orthodox Christians includes the priesthood).

Equality for women must therefore include a respect for their difference. In his 1995 *Letter to Women*, for example, John Paul called for changes to make women's equality a reality in the world: not just equal pay for equal work, but protections for working mothers; women who chose to have children, for example, should not be penalized in their careers for that choice. And he called for women who are "present and active in every area of life — social, economic, cultural, artistic, and political" — to help develop "a culture which unites reason and feeling" and "economic and political structures ever more worthy of humanity."

In a letter to Gertrude Mongella, secretary-general of the 1995 U.N. conference on women, John Paul II noted that "history is written almost exclusively as the narrative of men's achievements, when in fact its better part is most often moulded by women's determined and persevering action for good." He said the solution to the pressing questions facing women must be based "on the recognition of the inherent, inalienable dignity of women, and the importance of women's presence and participation in all aspects of social life."

A key dividing line between the "new" feminism advanced by Catholic women and its secular counterpart is the woman's "right to choose" on abortion. Because abortion remains an icon of the women's rights movement, the Catholic Church's opposition to it, in this narrative, makes the Church an enemy of the women's movement.

But the new feminists oppose abortion and contraception not only because these are wrong (see Chapter 6), but because these so-called gains for women, in reality, entrap them further within structures that compound their lack of freedom. New feminists believe that true solidarity with women requires that the underlying causes which make a child unwanted be challenged, not presumed. As John Paul II put it in *Evangelium Vitae* ("The Gospel of Life"): "There will never be justice, including equality, development and peace, for women or for men, unless there is an unfailing determination to respect, protect, love, and serve life — every human life, at every stage, and in every situation."

This ambition, of working for a civilization in which life is welcomed and protected, is the real route to women's freedom. For a woman to abort a child is to deny her own nature as a protector of growth and enabler of life. Abortion perpetuates the trap laid for women (as well as for men) in the Fall — of seeking an escape from loneliness by looking to men rather than God. By aborting, they remain locked in a cycle of destruction — of themselves and of new life.

A third tenet of the new feminism is the idea of the collaboration of the sexes. Where some twentieth-century feminism sees men and women as rivals, locked in a power struggle, new feminism regards the two genders as called to allow each other to become more fully who they are intended to be — as expressions of God's nature. As John Paul II says in his 1995 *Letter to Women*: "Womanhood and manhood are complementary not only from the physical and psychological points of view, but also from the ontological. It is only through the duality of the 'masculine' and the 'feminine' that the 'human' finds full realization."

Lastly, the new feminism calls for the integration of the feminine into contemporary society as a key to creating a more human, just and caring world. In *Evangelium Vitae*, John Paul II wrote that women occupied a "unique and decisive" role in transforming culture. "It depends on them," he added, "to promote a 'new feminism' which rejects the temptation of imitating models of 'male domination,' in order to acknowledge and affirm the true genius of women in every aspect of the life of society, and overcome all discrimination, violence and exploitation."

The key contribution of that "feminine genius," derived from women's capacity for motherhood, was to learn and then teach others that a person is loved and recognized because of the dignity which comes from being a person and not from other considerations, such as strength, beauty, or intelligence. This is the contribution, said John Paul II, "which the Church and humanity expect from women. And it is the indispensable prerequisite for an authentic cultural change."

John Paul II saw women as possessing naturally a contemplative outlook which grasps the utter gratuitousness of life — that all is a gift of God. This contemplative or spiritual outlook is in contrast to a (perverted male) mentality which seeks to commodify, possess, and conquer. The challenge, he went on, was "that of upholding, indeed strengthening, woman's role in the family while at the same time making it possible for her to use all her talents and exercise all her rights in building up society."

The pope concluded that the greater participation of women in society and public life is not just a matter of justice, but of necessity.

Women will increasingly play a part in the solution of the serious problems of the future: leisure time, quality of life, migration, social services, euthanasia, drugs, health care, the ecology, etc. In all these areas a greater presence of women in society will prove most valuable, for it will help to manifest the contradictions present when society is organized solely according to the criteria of efficiency and productivity, and it will force systems to be redesigned in a way which favors the processes of humanization which mark the "civilization of love."

☸

Existing Frame

"The gains for women in the twentieth century were achieved in spite of the legacy of Christianity, which has throughout its history oppressed women while lauding them as virgins and mothers. The Catholic Church continues that patriarchal legacy today by maintaining a gender ban on the priesthood, which sends a message to Catholic women

of inferiority. The Church has also been the most vociferous opponent of the Pill and abortion, two of the greatest gains in women's struggle to gain control of their fertility. If the Church were serious about the equal dignity of women, it would open up its structures to them. But it prefers to tell them to go off and be good wives and mothers."

REFRAME

The energy and spirit behind the emancipation of women come from Christianity, which recognized their equal dignity and transformed their roles. The history of the Church and women has been a mixed one, and the Church has not been immune from patriarchy. But women have played and continue to play a vital role in the Church's leadership and ministries. To claim that because women cannot be priests, therefore they have been excluded from power is to misunderstand both priesthood and the Church. Only priests can be men not because women are less, but because Jesus wished to create a new model of male authority. The emancipation of women has been recognized and encouraged by the modern Church as well as in it: there are far more women in leadership roles in the Church than in comparative institutions. But equality must not be attained at the expense of what makes women different. The particular gifts and capacities of women are needed both in the Church and in society in order to humanize and transform society. Not all women are called to be mothers; but their capacity for life-bearing differentiates women from men, which is why abortion is not the icon of female emancipation, but the sign of its failure. Inspired by John Paul II, the Church is at the vanguard of a new feminism which seeks to unleash what makes women unique and necessary.

௸

Key Messages

- Christianity laid the foundations for the modern emancipation of women by insisting on their equal worth and dignity. The early Church opened up new horizons for women, including social and public roles, although social pressures closed many down.
- Women have always played a vital, irreplaceable role in the life of the Church and continue to today.
- Although the Church, along with other institutions, has been

too slow in overcoming barriers to excluding women, nowadays it compares very favorably with secular society in the numbers of women in decision-making roles.

- Women cannot be priests, not because the Church regards them as unfit, but because Christ intended the priesthood to be male. To see this as discrimination is a category error.
- Inspired by Pope John Paul II's thinking, modern Catholic women have pioneered a "new feminism," one that seeks to emancipate women while safeguarding their distinct identity.
- The Catholic Church believes that women are necessary to humanize the structures of our society and economy. Without women playing a greater part in public life, society cannot become a better place.

Chapter 10

TEN PRINCIPLES OF CIVIL COMMUNICATION

Here are the ten principles which helped Catholic Voices develop the mind-set needed for this work:

1. Look for the positive intention behind the criticism.

Rather than the arguments you are going to face, consider the value that those arguments appeal to. Look for the (sometimes buried) Christian ethic behind the value. Which other (Christian) values is the critic ignoring, or has he not properly taken into account? Issues become neuralgic when they are about absolutes; clashes — like wars — happen when those absolute values appear threatened. That's what produces defensiveness and antagonism.

Rather than fall into this trap, consider the various values at stake and how they are to be weighed against each other. Then consider how, very early in the discussion, you can appeal to the value your critic is upholding. This has a disarming effect and frees both of you up for a calmer, considered discussion. You're no longer a warrior in a cultural battle for absolutes, but one bringing breadth and wisdom to a contentious issue.

Sometimes the value you uncover will not be a shared Christian value, but one directly at odds with the Christian conception. In many of the discussions about the state and society, for example, you may find yourself up against an individualistic or utilitarian viewpoint. But the principle still applies: it's important to understand the value involved — and if you can, to name it — and show that there are underlying principles at stake.

The purpose of the positive-intention exercise is to be able to distinguish between primary and secondary matters; our reasoning starts from our deep-seated values and moves to secondary considerations. Being able to distinguish the two, both in our own arguments and those of others, frees both sides up.

2. Shed light, not heat.

As people of faith we want to shed light on the difficult topics — enough heat has already been generated. But we also want to represent in ourselves and in our manner the Church we belong to and which has formed us.

If you come to the discussion to shed light rather than heat, your emphasis will be completely different. You will be a keen listener to the other's views and opinions, however much you disagree. Your objective will be to let chinks of light into the subject, to open up the discussion, to respect their views while holding your own.

Just as you can "catch" faith by witnessing the lives of people of faith who impress you, so you can catch "light" in an argument. Staying calm always works.

3. People won't remember what you said as much as how you made them feel.

Intellectuals and theologians, beware. Erudition is the opposite of communication, which uses simple words to explain complex ideas. It's not just about the lucidity of your arguments. It's about the effect that your words have on others.

Of course the truth of what you say matters. The purpose of being a Catholic Voice is above all to clarify. What we set out to do in responding to questions or criticisms is to shed light where there is currently darkness and confusion. But it is not *we* who persuade; it is the Truth. Our task is to serve the Truth the best we can. And we serve Truth best when we do not try to "defeat" those who object. Aim for civility, empathy, and clarity.

Deft rhetorical maneuvers and point-scoring can be excellent games, but they do not illuminate. A vigorous debate is unlikely to alter perceptions. The danger is that you will "win" the argument and lose the audience, whether two or (in a TV news broadcast) two million people.

Evaluate, therefore, after each exchange, according to one criterion alone: Did I help others understand better the Church's teaching or positions? And how did I make everyone feel? Uplifted, or battered? Inspired, or harried? Anxious to hear more, or relieved I stopped?

4. Show, don't tell.

This foundational principle of good writing applies to communication generally. People prefer stories to lectures, and are more convinced by experience than abstract argument. That doesn't mean you shouldn't use arguments — this book is full of them. But where you can, supplement them with illustrations: anecdotes from personal experience, or hypothetical situations which help people to "imagine" what you are trying to say. Rather than tell someone that the Church assists AIDS sufferers in Africa, tell them about the hospitals and dispensaries in the remotest villages in the African countryside where nuns care for patients in ramshackle huts. Rather than say we need more hospices — which are vague, unknown institutions to most people — paint the picture of places where the dying are helped and reassured, and invite people to imagine what it would be like if we had more of them. Think of yourself not as the spokesman of a remote corporation, but as a delighted disciple with stories and experiences to share.

5. Think in triangles.

Discussions can be very disorganized, meandering down various blind alleys until the whole theme of the discussion is lost. Make sure your contribution is concise and clear and doesn't lead anyone else off the beaten track. Hone your thoughts down to the three important points you want to make. It's very unusual for you to be able to make them all; if you can get two out of three into the discussion you'll be doing well. But it's important for you to marshal your thoughts into the three points.

See them as a triangle. Whenever you are in a discussion think how it relates to the triangle. Then bring in your point. Don't get distracted by other people into abandoning your points; don't wait for the "right" moment to make your points; simply identify where the discussion is in relation to the points on your triangle.

Although the "key messages" at the end of each chapter are more than three, you'll find these a useful place to identify your triangle. At least one of those points should address the positive intention behind the criticism. Having made it allows you then to proceed to the other two points.

6. Be positive.

This is a baseline communication principle, and doubly important when we are making the Church's case *against* something. The Church *is* against many things, but only because it is *for* so much more — there is much it wishes to protect and enhance. Almost everything the Church says is because it wants to call people — and society in general — to fullness of life, health, and sustainable prosperity. The Church is not a grim-faced moral policeman; it is more like Mother Teresa, tending to the world's forgotten and ailing people, and it is worth holding up that image when you speak of the Church's teaching. Experience — of prayer, reflection on Scripture, and centuries of deep immersion into humanity's deepest struggles — have made the Church an "expert in humanity." It offers a series of signposts which highlight the wrong turns and dead ends on the road to human flourishing, both in the lives of individuals and in the architecture of society.

Being positive is not about smiling and being "nice." It is about bringing the discussion back to the positive vision the Church has for people — the endless, wonderful possibilities of our freedom. Catholic Voices should be idealists and radicals, inviting society to another, better way. Pro-lifers should sound like anti-slavery campaigners, not admonishing moralists, just as opponents of assisted dying should be campaigners for hospices on every corner. Don't be a grim reaper; be the angel that points to the brighter horizon.

7. Be compassionate.

Compassion is a quality for which Christians are meant to be famous, yet which is sadly often missing in a discussion with a Catholic. The main reason is covered above, in the positive-intention point: we feel that our most treasured values are threatened. People who care passionately are often frustrated with others who appear to be dismissing or ignoring what is important to them. Yet that frustration is essentially self-centered. You are demanding that another understands and values what you regard as important. But the critic is also someone who regards what he or she believes as important, and is likely to be frustrated that you do not value that. A vicious cycle is set up.

Learning to be compassionate, even in heated exchanges, is key to breaking out of this cycle of mutual rebuke. Underneath almost all of the neuralgic issues treated in this book are deeply personal ethical questions: ones of sexuality, dying, illness, belief. It is very likely that the person you are in discussion with has had direct experience of the neuralgic issue, either personally, or witnessing firsthand; or has an experience of authority and institutions that have left them hurt. You may or may not know that they have had that experience; if not, you should assume it. God is a common scapegoat for anger, a lightning rod for otherwise unfocused frustrations. Being compassionate is about understanding this anger and hurt, and relating to it, as one human being to another.

Critics of the Church are particularly sensitive to Catholics appearing robotically to repeat what they have been "told" to think. Personal experience is opposed to institutional orthodoxy, the experience of individual victims is counterposed to the collective interest, and so on. In these contrapositions, the Catholic always comes off worse — not least because putting people before institutions is at the heart of Christianity itself. There is a prejudice that the Church operates by pumping out papal diktats hungrily consumed by people anxious to avoid thinking for themselves. But more important is the notion — we might even call it a positive intention — that it is experience that carries the greatest authority.

How to avoid appearing the cold, callous representative of a distant human institution is a constant challenge for Catholic Voices. There are many ways of stepping away from this trap: speaking from experience yourself, telling stories which also appeal to emotion, or providing counterexamples. But it may be that sometimes we simply need to be good listeners, ready to absorb the anger and hurt that some people have with the Church; that in itself is a valuable compassionate tool. If it is their first experience of being listened to by a person of faith, compassion is the most valuable witness we can offer.

8. Check your facts, but avoid robotics.

Part of good preparation is marshaling helpful facts and figures that reframe the discussion. But remember that statistics can appear abstract and inhuman, or a cover: politicians using them are usually thought to be lying. Above all avoid statistical ping-pong. If you must use statistics, keep them simple. Make sure that your figures are on the point and clear—and expressed in human, clear language: not 30 out of a 100 people, but "one in three"; and not "25 percent" but "a quarter." Use them only when they say what needs to be said, not simply as reinforcements.

Criticisms of the Church are often based on a misquotation or lack of understanding of the complete picture. So it's important to go to the sources and see where the truth has been twisted or imperfectly grasped. Remember the bigger picture: priest numbers in the United States are far lower than they were thirty years ago, but still more (relative to numbers of Catholics) than almost anywhere in the world. A fact is meaningless without context and perspective.

Remember, too, that you can't say everything; time —and attention spans — are limited. Focus on what's to the point, and important. Leave less important issues for later.

9. It's not about you.

Good communication is essentially about putting the ego in the back seat. It's not *you* that the critic is failing to value or respect; it's what you represent. Your fear, self-consciousness, and defensiveness are the products of your protesting ego. Think of John the Baptist, a fearless communicator; his strength came from knowing that he was the glass door through which people would come to Christ.

So let's nail this question of whether you are going to give a fantastic or dreadful performance. A certain degree of nervousness before speaking in public is inevitable. The adrenalin helps you focus. But excessive nervousness is often a sign of self-consciousness. Remember, people are not interested in what *you* think; they are interested in what you *think*.

The ego however tricks us into believing that *we* are the focus, which makes us alternately jittery with nerves, or puffed up with an absurd pride. If you're nervous, you might jabber, trying to get all your points out at once. Take a few deep breaths to calm down before you start and pause before you answer. The best way of stilling nerves, of course, is to prepare well.

Praying before entering the studio or a debate is vital: not just to calm the nerves and to put the ego in the backseat, but also to remember who and what this is for. Pray for the Holy Spirit to be with you and speaking through you. And try the Catholic Voices prayer at the end of this chapter.

If it does go badly, rejoice! Success has almost nothing to teach us. Ask someone you trust to go through it with you and see where you went wrong and where you could improve. This is where learning happens, and be glad of the lesson.

And remember: this is much less important than you think. And you were certainly not as bad as you thought.

You are doing God's work and trying your best. That is always enough, even if it goes badly. The ego would like to persuade us that we are either the world's greatest orator, or the most wretched creature ever to be dragged before a microphone. The truth is that we are neither, and mostly quite good. Settle for that.

10. Witnessing, not winning.

One of the journalists assigned to cover the papal trip was relaxing in a London pub after covering Benedict XVI's second day in London. At the table next to him were two young women who were looking up without much interest at the live coverage of the pope arriving in Hyde Park. Two articulate, passionate, young Catholic Voices were being interviewed and giving commentary, explaining, concisely and joyfully, what the pope meant to them, to Catholics, and to the United Kingdom; and why they regarded the trip as beneficial for society as a whole. After they had finished, one young woman in the pub turned to the other and said: "Well, I suppose they're not all crazy, then." The American journalist told us: "Looks like you hit a home run there."

The power of these reactions is not something that is easy to gauge. But many people who come back to the Church after many years away, or who decide to inquire about becoming Catholic, will often cite hearing someone or seeing someone saying something that struck them, and which nagged at them.

Mostly, though, it's not the result of a dazzling argument or a beautiful turn of a phrase. Mostly it's a "reframing": a prejudice or preconception is challenged, or even reversed. We call this "conversion." The model is Saint Paul, who turned from a persecutor of Christians to the most famous of Christ's witnesses. His conversion involved a new way of seeing. Having been scandalized by Christianity, and wanting to destroy it, he came to see that what scandalized him was none other than the Truth.

Inviting people to see the Church differently by communicating the truth about it is what Catholic Voices exists for.

In the Introduction we spoke of the way the Catholic faith "scandalizes": it causes people to react strongly and ask hard questions. We noted how a *skandalon* is an obstacle in the path. It causes people to stop and think, and question. And that can be the start of another path, one that leads, potentially, to a new way of looking at something. Or it can lead to the "turning away" which Jesus warns of. The task of Catholic Voices is to insert ourselves into precisely that moment, that moment of scandal when people have not yet turned away completely, but are indignant, or confused, or curious. Every challenge to us is an opportunity to witness: clarifying misunderstanding, shedding light where there is myth and confusion, demonstrating empathy and compassion and a deeper vision.

The enemy of such a witness is a desire to "win" and "defeat." An attitude of rivalry and victory, of winners and losers, of "us and them," of "right and wrong" — this is the language of battles and sieges, of war and persecution. There are not a few Catholics who want to take up cudgels on behalf of a pope they believe to be unfairly maligned on issues such as gay adoption or clerical sex abuse. But while they are right to want to defend him, and to put the record straight, they have to avoid being part of the same cycle of accusation and defense.

As a model, take Jesus in the Gospel of John: endlessly harried and challenged, he never falls into the attitude of a persecuted victim.

No one stands outside that cycle better than Pope Benedict himself. What did he do, after landing in Scotland? He praised Britain, gave thanks for the hospitality, kissed babies, and melted hearts. He had strong words — scandalous words — for his listeners; but they were words of reason, compassion, and conviction. He did not command, but appealed. He showed compassion, empathy, and real love. But because he had first witnessed, the British people were ready to listen. That was his victory, and it's the only kind we should seek.

Catholic Voices Prayer

God our Father,
Bless and guide all those involved in Catholic Voices.
Give us the gifts of the Holy Spirit that we need for this work,
especially wisdom, gentleness, courage, and joy.
Help us to be faithful to Christ and to his Church,
and to be open to the questions that people bring us.
Help us to love and respect all those we meet.
Support us in our difficulties and setbacks.
May our words and the witness of our lives
give you glory and help others to be more open to you.
We make this prayer through Christ our Lord. Amen.

Our Lady, Seat of Wisdom, pray for us.
St. Francis de Sales, pray for us.
Blessed Titus Brandsma, pray for us.
Blessed Cardinal Newman, pray for us.